0010012886

GW00993015

Making Assessment Work

LEARNING AND INFORMATION
SERVICES
CHARLOTTE MASON
LIBRARY
AMBLESIDE

Values and principles
in assessing
young children's learning

Mary Jane Drummond
Dorothy Rouse
Gillian Pugh

© Nottingham Group & National Children's Bureau, 1992

Making Assessment Work

Values and principles in assessing young children's learning

ACKNOWLEDGEMENTS

This pack of learning materials is the result of educators from many different settings, and from many different regions, working together to 'Make Assessment Work'. Without their collaboration, their contributions, comments, cautions and encouragement, this pack would look very different.

We would like to thank the members of the project group for their key role in developing this pack from the original draft proposal, for helping with the organisation of the trialling groups, and for commenting on the trial version.

PROJECT GROUP

Joy Bell	NNEB course tutor, Leicester College of Further Education
Iram Siraj-Blatchford	Lecturer in early years education, University of Warwick
Pamela Calder	Senior lecturer, South Bank Polytechnic
June Fitzgibbon	Tutor, Nursery Nurses College of Further Education, Bristol
Pat Jefferson	Early years adviser, North Tyneside
Joan Lister	Headteacher, Ashfield Nursery School, Newcastle-upon-Tyne
Shirley Maxwell	Tutor in early childhood education, Froebel Institute
Cathy Nutbrown	Area coordinator: early childhood education, Sheffield
Nimet Rener	Training and development consultant, formerly High Scope development officer
Wendy Scott	Primary inspector, Royal Borough of Kensington & Chelsea
Olivia Vincenti	Manager, Curtis Family Centre, Barnet
Dorothy Wedge	County adviser, Services to the Under Fives, Cambridgeshire
Sheila Wolfendale	Professor, psychology department, Polytechnic of East London

This project developed over three years from January 1990 to September 1992 and was supported by funding from the Department For Education. During August 1991, 100 copies of the trial version were distributed to people who had offered or had been approached to organise piloting of the material with groups of students and practitioners on inservice and initial training courses.

Over 30 groups and many individuals and organisations gave us detailed comments and their help is gratefully acknowledged here. Thank you all for your time and your observations.

TRIAL GROUPS

P. Athey, educational psychologist, Essex
Inservice - nursery class, special school, nursery class.

Joy Bell, further education tutor, Leicestershire.
DPQS students from group day care, family centres, nursery schools, nursery classes, primary schools and special schools.

Sandra Brown, advisory teacher, Harrow
Inservice - nursery centre, reception class.

David Carroll, education psychologist, Bedfordshire
Inservice - group day care, nursery school, nursery class, primary school, support teams, educational psychologists.

Liz Cowley, development officer, National Children's Bureau.
Australian Early Childhood Association.
International Family Day Care Organisation.
Theological training course, West Midlands.
Inspection Unit, social services, Leicestershire.
Advisors, social services, Oxfordshire and Cambridgeshire.

Audrey Curtis, university lecturer, London Institute of Education.
MA and Diploma students.

Mary Jane Drummond, tutor in primary education, Cambridge Institute of Education. Inservice - early years practitioners, East Anglia.

June Fitzgibbon, nursery nurse tutor, Bristol.
NNEB students.

Noirin Hayes, tutor, Dublin Institute of Technology, Ireland.
Students, National Certificate in Pre-School Care and group day care.

Gena Houston, NNEB course tutor, the College of North East London.
NNEB students.

Penny Holding, education psychologist, Tower Hamlets.
Inservice - nursery school, nursery class, advisory teacher, educational psychologist.

Sue Jackson, nursery teacher, Surrey.
Inservice - nursery school, nursery class, primary school, primary diagnostic unit.

Tricia Kent, ex-nursery headteacher, Cornwall.
Inservice - family centre, nursery school, primary school, under fives advisors, social services, under fives coordinator, health visitor.

Joan Lister, nursery headteacher, Newcastle upon Tyne.
Inservice - nursery school.

Jenny Manning, headteacher, Cambridgeshire.
Nursery school.

Patricia Morris, educational psychologist, teachers' centre, Hillingdon.
Inservice - nursery class, primary school, nursery for children with 'severe learning difficulties'.

Jeannette Nowrung, playgroup leader, Norfolk.
Inservice - playgroup staff.

Cathy Nutbrown, area coordinator for early childhood, Sheffield.
Inservice - parent and toddler group, nursery class, primary school, advisory teachers, playgroups, school governors.

Jennifer Pozzani, advisory teacher, London Borough of Hillingdon.
Inservice - family centre, nursery school, nursery class, primary school.

Dorothy Rouse, development officer, National Children's Bureau.
Inservice - group day care, nursery school, special school, family centre, combined nursery centre, in Camden, Islington, City, and Kensington and **Chelsea**. Managers of orphanages, Romania.

Sue Sayers, educational psychologist, Surrey.
Inservice - group day care, nursery school, primary school, special school.

Jenni Smith, educational psychologist, Brent.
Inservice - under fives family centre.

Lynsi Smith, further education tutor, Hertfordshire.
Students - International diploma in Childcare for multi-professionals in Asian countries.

Jan Seabourne, primary teacher, Suffolk.
Inservice - primary school, nursery class.

Michele Ward, educational psychologist, London Borough of Newham.
Inservice - nursery school.

Judy Warner, Day care adviser, Social Services, Warwickshire.
Inservice - playgroup, childminder, private day nursery.

Janine Wooster, coordinator: pre-school home visiting team, children with special needs, London Borough of Newham.
Inservice - group day care, family centre, family day care, playgroup, nursery class, nursery school, primary school, pre-school special needs team.

COMMENTS AND CONTRIBUTIONS WERE GENEROUSLY GIVEN BY:

Anne Blackwell	Educational psychologist, Essex
Jenny Colls	Infant teacher, Cambridgeshire
Tricia David	Lecturer in early years education, University of Warwick
Julie Dent	Preschool Playgroups Association, Warwickshire
Peter Dreghorn	Divisional education officer (Primary), Strathclyde, Scotland
Peter Elfer	Senior development officer, Early Childhood Unit, National Children's Bureau
Jean Ensing	HMI, Department for Education
Macy Gait	Headteacher, South Glamorgan, Wales
Sheila Gatiss	Development officer, The Council for Disabled Children, National Children's Bureau
Marilyn Halpin	Pre-school Playgroups Association, Newcastle-upon-Tyne
Margaret Hanney	Head, Early Childhood Unit, National Children's Bureau, Wales
Sonya Hinton	Educational psychologist, Guildford
Annette Holman	Regional adviser, Pre-Fives Services, Strathclyde, Scotland
Pam Lafferty	Development officer, High/Scope UK
Jane Lane	Senior Executive Officer, Education Section, Commission for Racial Equality
Margaret Martin	Day care advisor, social services, Warwickshire
Hannah Mortimer	Educational psychologist, North Yorkshire Education Department
Judith Nasatyr	Educational psychologist, London Borough of Hillingdon
Ann Robinson	Information officer, Early Childhood Unit, National Children's Bureau
Madge Scarse	Advisory teacher, early years, Suffolk
Dr Susan Shepherd	Department of Health
Maureen Smith	Senior assistant director, NNEB
Brenda Staniland	Staff Inspector, Department for Education
Philippa Stobbs	Development officer, The Council for Disabled Children, National Children's Bureau
Alison Warn	Primary headteacher, Hertfordshire

We would like to thank Catherine Murphy, Julie Smith, Wendy Ebden and Tracey Coates at NES Arnold for helping us to design this pack, and to Fiona Blakemore, Publications Manager at the National Children's Bureau for her support. Thank you to Clare Davies-Jones for her illustrations to these materials.

Very warm thanks to Penny Collyer at the Cambridge Institute of Education (CIE) and to Anita Udoh and Patricia Thomas at the National Children's Bureau for typing the successive drafts of 'Making Assessment Work'. Thanks to Claire Johnson at the CIE for her work in photocopying the 100 trial copies.

Last but not least, thank you to Fared, Heloise, Horst, Guljeet, James, Alice, Joey, Bevan and to all the other children whose play, talk, thinking, living and learning have been described in this pack; they will help us all to 'Make Assessment Work' for all young children.

Mary Jane Drummond	**Dorothy Rouse**	**Gillian Pugh**
Tutor in Primary Education	Development Officer	Early Childhood Unit Director
Cambridge Institute of Education	Early Childhood Unit	National Children's Bureau
	National Children's Bureau	

June 1992

Making
Assessment
Work

CONTENTS

INTRODUCTION

BEING A GROUP LEADER

Making
Assessment
Work

INTRODUCTION

WHY HAS THIS PACK BEEN DEVELOPED?

This pack has been written to support all those who work with young children in the process of reviewing, discussing and developing their ideas about observation, assessment and record-keeping in the early years. The authors of the pack believe that effective assessment of children's learning can and should play a vital part in the provision of quality care and education. The pack is based on the view that assessment is a process in which our understanding of children's learning, acquired through observation and reflection, can be made to work for the children's benefit; it can be used to evaluate and enrich the whole of the curriculum we offer in the early years. The activities in the pack have been written to help early years workers, in whatever setting, to think about the complex issues that surround this central idea: the idea of 'making assessment work' .... for children and for children's learning.

THE AIMS OF THE PACK

The aims of the pack are to help all educators of young children:

- to be clearer about the system of values and beliefs that underlies the process of assessment

- to understand more clearly the emotional dimension of assessment, for everyone involved - parents, children and educators

- to think about how what they know about children's learning must be taken into account in their assessment practices

- to review and develop their observation skills and techniques, to explore ways in which observation can become part of their daily routines, and to think about ways of involving parents in this process

- to establish the basic principles that will guide and inform their assessment practices

- to think about how assessment can be used to review provision as a whole, to plan for individual children, and to identify the next steps in their own learning

- to create or update an effective written format for record-keeping and for transferring records to other educators

- to be clearer about the ways in which assessment can be made to work for the benefit of all children, whatever their special learning needs and abilities, in the context of their ethnicity, culture and heritage

The pack does not attempt to provide a step-by-step guide to observation and assessment in the early years. This would not

Making
Assessment
Work

INTRODUCTION

be a realistic undertaking, or even a very useful one. Following other people's instructions is rarely the first step in learning to think for oneself. Spending time thinking about difficult issues in assessment may, in the long run, be more worthwhile for early years educators than trying to follow a prescriptive approach to particular practices. The purpose of the pack is to encourage those who use it to think about what they do and why they do it; it is intended to support a process of critical enquiry and reflection, not to encourage a hunt for instant solutions and right answers.

Throughout the pack, there are opportunities to think about issues of inequality and discrimination, and the ways in which children's lives may be affected by adult attitudes towards ethnic origin, class, gender, culture, religion, language and disability. All early years educators, including those working in predominantly or all White areas within our multicultural society, have a responsibility to identify and challenge racist, sexist and other discriminatory attitudes and practices.

WHO IS THE PACK INTENDED FOR?

Care and education for young children are offered in a wide variety of settings, staffed by a range of people with different training and experience. The Rumbold Report brought an element of unity to this rich diversity by adopting the term 'educator' to describe any adult working with young children, in whatever setting. The authors of this pack have followed this practice, and the pack is intended for all educators of children from birth to eight.

These educators may be working closely with children, in day-by-day settings (people such as playgroup leaders, nursery nurses, childminders and teachers); or they may be part of a more extended family of educators, who work with children as and when the need arises (people such as educational psychologists, health visitors, and speech therapists).

For ways in which the pack can be used see pages 11-12.

WHAT DO WE MEAN BY ASSESSMENT?

In recent years, especially since the implementation of the 1988 Education Reform Act, the term 'assessment' has come to suggest an objective, mechanical process of measurement. It suggests checklists, precision, explicit criteria, incontrovertible facts and figures. In this pack, the term is used in a different sense.

When we work with young children, when we play and talk with them, when we watch them and everything they do, we are witnessing a fascinating and inspiring process: we are seeing young children learn. As we think about what we see, and try to understand it, we have embarked on the process that in this pack we label 'assessment'. We are using the

Making
Assessment
Work

term to describe the ways in which, in our everyday practice, we observe children's learning, strive to understand it, and then put our understanding to good use.

Young children's awesome capacity for learning imposes a massive responsibility on the educators whose task is to support, enrich and extend that learning. We cannot know if we are successful in this task, unless we carefully monitor the learning that takes place before our eyes. We cannot provide quality care and education unless we assess the quality of children's learning, in groups and as individuals. The urgent task of evaluating the services we provide for young children, especially during a time of change and development in response to recent legislation, necessarily includes an evaluation of the effect of these services on the young children themselves.

In assessment, we can appreciate and understand what children learn about themselves, about the world around them, about their place in the world. By monitoring this learning, we can recognise their achievements, and their individuality, the differences between them. We can use our assessments to shape and enrich our curriculum, our interactions, our provision as a whole; we can use assessment as a way of identifying what children will be able to learn next, so that we can support and extend that learning. Assessment is part of our daily practice in striving for quality.

ASSESSMENT IN THE EARLY YEARS: THE CONTEXT

This pack has been written at a time when the whole issue of assessment of children's learning has become the subject of heated public debate. If this debate is to have worthwhile consequences for young children, it is essential for all those who work with young children to have a voice in it.

Part of this debate has been triggered by increased public concern about reports of falling standards, especially in reading, reports which are both hotly contested and widely publicised. Part of it is a response to the new emphasis on parents' right of choice in their children's education, established in the 1988 Education Reform Act. The right to choose inevitably leads parents to make comparisons between schools, and the claims that schools make for themselves. The local management of schools, another provision of the 1988 Act, has made governors and headteachers acutely aware of the financial implications of falling rolls; increased competitiveness between schools is a real possibility, and forms of assessment that show each school in its most favourable light will certainly play a part in that competition. The increase of educational provision in the private sector is another factor in the current debate: parents who pay for services have a legitimate interest in knowing that they are getting good value for their money.

Within the education service, the impact of recent legislation on the process of assessment has been dramatic. Under the

Making
Assessment
Work

INTRODUCTION

1988 Education Reform Act, there is a statutory requirement for teachers of six and seven-year-olds to assess their pupils' learning in two different ways. First, teachers are required to make continuous 'Teacher Assessments' of each child's learning, using as a measure the 'attainment targets' laid down in the National Curriculum.

Secondly, they are required to assess their pupils' learning in Mathematics, English and Science by means of 'Standard Assessment Tasks', commonly known as SATs. Here too, the teachers must measure each child's performance on the tasks against the pre-defined attainment targets.

In both forms of assessment, (teacher assessment and SATs) the teacher must assign each child's performance on each attainment target to one of three levels of achievement. Through a complicated mathematical process, the levels found for each child are aggregated to give overall levels for Maths, English and Science, (Level One, Two or Three), which must be reported to each child's parents.

The storm of controversy that has surrounded these requirements since they were first announced, and that has continued through the piloting (in 1990) and the first national trial (during the summer of 1991), has raised awareness of a whole range of difficult questions about how and why we should assess children's learning. Assessment has always been a complex and problematic process; the requirements of the 1988 Education Reform Act have thrown up new difficulties, new tensions, even, perhaps, new possibilities.

Those who work with the youngest children in school, with four or five-year-olds in reception classes, or with even younger children in nursery classes, playgroups and day nurseries have also been affected by the 1988 Act. Especially in primary schools, as the National Curriculum takes root in established practice, the curriculum offered to children of non-statutory age has inevitably changed; in the interests of continuity and progression, teachers of young children have learned to draw on the statutory programmes of study, and to take account of the forms of assessment being developed for six and seven-year-olds. Many of these teachers feel that they are being pressured to adopt ways of working that are more appropriate for older children; some of them feel that their cherished and distinctive 'early years' practice is being threatened; all of them are aware of the need to articulate clearly and confidently the principles and purposes of their own practices in assessing children's learning.

The 1989 Children Act, too, with its emphasis on the welfare and rights of children, and on the need to work in partnership with parents, will have its effect on approaches to assessment. One of the requirements of the Act is for a joint review of all forms of provision for children under eight to be carried out every three years, by social services and education departments.

INTRODUCTION

This review, mainly concerned with the quantity and types of services provided, will be supplemented by an annual inspection of the quality of the provision in private and voluntary nurseries. The Children Act recommends that social services departments should turn to local education authorities for support and guidance with registration and inspection: one of the more positive spin-offs from the Act should therefore be increased collaboration between social services and education departments, working together on questions of curriculum, evaluation and assessment.

The Act also requires local authorities to provide day care and other services for children 'in need', including children with disabilities; this too will require education, social services and health professionals to work with each other and with parents in assessing and meeting children's needs.

The authoritative 'Rumbold Report', the report of the Committee of Inquiry into the quality of educational experiences offered to three and four-year-olds (DES 1990), has played an important part in helping those who work with young children to see more clearly the general issues that affect them all. The report reviews the characteristics that all young children have in common, and builds on this description to establish a set of aims for early childhood education, and the outline of a curriculum for the under-fives. The Report emphasises the importance of a broad range of experiences in developing young children's abilities, and warns against possibly harmful influences on the early years curriculum:

'We believe that...educators should guard against pressures which might lead them to over-concentrate on formal teaching and upon the attainment of a specific set of targets' (DES 1990 paragraph 66).

The report sees two key criteria for quality as 'collaborative planning which is based upon systematic and regular observation-based assessment of children in all areas of development; and record-keeping which is built upon contributions from the educator, parent and child, and which feeds and supports children's learning' (p.35).

Finally, the introduction of a system of national vocational qualifications for day care and early education workers in January 1992, and the publication of national standards against which these workers will be assessed (Care Sector Consortium 1991), have focused attention on the need for all who work with young children to be skilled in 'observing and assessing the development and behaviour of the children' (Unit C.11). This requirement underlines the part that adults' understanding of children's learning must play in the provision of quality care and education.

It is against this background of parental, professional and public concern that this pack has been written by a multidisciplinary group of early years educators.
(A fuller discussion of these themes can be found in Pugh (ed) 1992).

Making Assessment Work

INTRODUCTION

'NOT FOR SALE'

In Section One of this pack, **Looking at values,** you will be invited to take part in an activity in which you will be asked to think about the few, the very few basic principles that we would never abandon. The authors of the pack have also worked to identify and clarify the principles that they believe underlie the practice of assessment in the early years. These principles are not negotiable; they are 'not for sale' in these discussion activities. The pack does not suggest that there is only one acceptable set of practices in assessment; but the practices that educators develop for themselves cannot add up to effective assessment unless they are based on a coherent set of principles. Your work on the pack will, the authors hope, enable you to establish both principles and practices. **Our** principles, to which **we** hold firm, are as follows.

First, the principle of respect. We believe that assessment must be carried out with a proper respect for the children themselves, for their parents and other carers, and for their educators. We must respect their ethnicity, their cultural heritage, their religions and the languages they speak. Our assessment practice must be respectful of all children, whatever their gifts, abilities or special learning needs. Our respect will be expressed in our actions, in our words and deeds, in our daily interactions, in our attitudes to children, their parents and our fellow educators. Our respect will be expressed by countering racist attitudes, words and deeds.

Secondly, the principle that the care and education of young children are not two separate, discrete activities. In our work as educators we both care and educate. **Quality care is educational; and quality education is caring**. As a consequence, when we assess young children, we will attend to the whole of their human development, not just to certain aspects of it. We will be attentive to children learning to love one another, as well as to children learning to count.

Thirdly, the principle of 'the loving use of power'. We believe it is important to acknowledge the power of the early years educator and to struggle to use it lovingly, wisely and well. (The theme of power is developed more fully in Section Two **About feelings**).

Our fourth principle is that the interests of children are paramount. Assessment is a process that must enhance their lives, their learning and their development. Assessment must work for children.

INTRODUCTION

The pack is subdivided into nine sections.

1. Looking at values
2. About feelings
3. Looking at learning
4. Observations
5. In search of principles
6. Principles into practice
7. Writing it down
8. Making it work
9. Passing it on

Some of these sections have titles that speak for themselves: **Looking at learning** and **Observations**, for example. You will not be surprised to find these topics in a pack on assessment. But two other sections may seem less self-explanatory; you may even wonder why they have been included. These are Section One **Looking at values** and Section Two **About feelings.** Before starting your work on the pack, it is important that you understand why these sections have been written, and the essential part they play in the pack as a whole.

LOOKING AT VALUES

Section One is based on the proposition that any form of assessment is based on an implicit value system, which is built up of beliefs about children, about what kinds of beings they are, what kinds of ways they should and do behave, what kinds of feelings they should and do have. A description of the ideal child, or the normal child, is not normally made explicit in the process of assessment. Nevertheless, as we set about observing and assessing young children, we do have, deep in our mind's eye, some dearly held beliefs about what we are looking for.

When we look at children, and interact with them, we interpret and make meaning of what we see, even if we aren't aware of what we're doing or how we do it. It's as if we store, behind our eyes, a million memories and half-forgotten incidents; and this storehouse of impressions and events inevitably affects our seeing, and our understanding.

I look at what they do

and I make meaning of it

She's tired

he's happy

WHAT CHILDREN DO ..

inside my head

Is all that I've learned about the world

FACTS   MORE FACTS

my own feelings

my own childhood

what other people say

Making Assessment Work

INTRODUCTION

If we could somehow turn around, and look at all that lies behind our eyes, that storehouse of learning would not disappear. But we might understand it more clearly. We might see some connections and contradictions. We might find out how we learned some of these things and why we store them so preciously.

This section of the pack invites you to do just that - to turn around and to look at yourself - your accumulated values, beliefs and feelings - so that we can learn more about how and why we see what we see when we look at children's learning.

ABOUT FEELINGS

The purpose of Section Two is to open up discussion about the emotional dimension of assessment - its effect on those being assessed and on those doing the assessment. The process of assessment is sometimes treated as if its outcomes were simple: raised standards, increased understanding, improved communication, more effective teaching and learning. This section suggests that there is a more human way of approaching assessment, in which we take into account our knowledge of ourselves as people with emotions, not just as educators with expertise. This section raises questions about children's feelings (and how we handle them), and about our own feelings. It emphasises the inescapable emotional involvement of both assessor and assessed in the complex process we are investigating in the pack.

USING THE PACK

The pack can be used by:

- all educators working with children from birth onwards, in any setting: in family day care or in group day care or in education

- mixed groups of educators from different backgrounds and services (health, education and social services, the voluntary and private sectors), possibly working in one locality (town, region, or social services district)

- groups of staff working in similar settings, for example, playgroup leaders in one district, or teachers and nursery nurses in a local education authority, or a group of childminders within a community

- a staff team in one nursery or group or centre; for example, all the staff in an infant school or day nursery or children's centre

- a committee, staff and parents in a playgroup or parent and toddler group

Making
Assessment
Work

- members of a local under-fives liaison group or community forum

- college tutors running post-experience and in-service training courses for early years educators

- teachers of older children, in primary or special schools

- parents and workers from a nursery or family centre

Although the pack is suitable for all educators of young children, it has been developed on the assumption that, in mixed disciplinary groups, educators have much to learn from one another. Many of the discussion activities will be more rewarding if they are carried out by practitioners from a range of backgrounds, with different experiences and expectations.

YOU COULD USE THIS PACK

- on a short but substantial in-service course (of, for example, twelve two-hour evening sessions)

- on award-bearing multi-disciplinary courses in early childhood studies

- on short informal courses of eight to ten meetings

- as support material for regular staff meetings, spread over a year or more, at which assessment was a constant theme or focus

YOU COULD USE SHORT EXTRACTS FROM THIS PACK

- on a one-day introductory course on assessment for local early years workers, as the starting point for further development work

- on a primary school's training day, as an introduction to issues of assessment

The activities in the pack have been designed for use in small groups of up to twelve people. If you have a much larger group (for example, at a day conference) you will need to break down into smaller groups to work on selected activities.

The role of the group leader is crucial to how the pack is used. Several of the activities require skilled intervention on the part of the group leader, and these have additional notes in the pack.

The next section **Being a group leader** contains some **Notes for group leaders,** on issues of organisation and management, and also some discussion activities that group leaders could use together. Many groups work well when the leadership is shared by two colleagues. This is often both helpful to the group and supportive to the group leaders.

REMEMBER: the purpose of the pack is to encourage participants to think about what, how, when and why they assess children's learning, rather than to identify fool-proof, sure-fire answers to the difficult questions they will meet as they work on the pack. The group leader's role is not to instruct, but to enable the group to participate, to think, to draw on their own experiences, to reflect and to learn. The activities have been designed to help this happen.

FINDING YOUR WAY THROUGH THE PACK

This introduction is followed by a preliminary section for group leaders: you will be able to decide for yourself how and when you will use this material in preparing for your work as a group leader. Depending on your previous experience, you may allocate a longer or shorter time, working alone or with others, to **Being a group leader.**

Sections 1-9, which form the main body of the pack, have been written to be used consecutively. Each section opens with an introduction, explaining the underlying principles and purposes of this part of the pack: you may want to photocopy these introductions, as you start work on each section, so that group members have an overview of how each section fits into the pack as a whole.

Each section consists of a number of activities. Sections 1, 2, 4, 8 and 9 (viz: **Looking at values, About feelings, Observations, Making it work, Passing it on**) contain a number of activities from which you may wish to make a selection.

In Sections 3, 5, 6, 7 (viz: **Looking at learning, In search of principles, Principles into practice, Writing it down**) the activities provided form a sequence that all group members will need to follow in order to develop a full understanding of the issues under consideration.

The pages describing each activity are to be photocopied for your group members. The purpose of each activity is explained in a brief introduction: you may want to copy these pages as well, or you may prefer to introduce the activity yourself, using your own words (or pictures). Handouts are provided for many activities, and you will need to photocopy these pages in advance. Details of everything that needs to be done in preparation are given before each activity.

Notes to Group Leaders

There are also occasional notes to group leaders: these are intended to help you look out for ways to challenge assumptions, misconceptions and taken-for-granted ways of thinking. They may help you to support your group members in the process of new or unexpected learning.

As you complete your work on each section of the pack, it will be worthwhile to spend a little time with your group reviewing your experiences with the materials you selected. You and your group members will want to think about the additional unexpected questions that have been raised for you, about what you have learned from your discussions with each other, and about your personal and emotional responses to the issues raised. It isn't necessary to spend long on this miniature review, but it will be a useful way of pulling together your work so far, before you embark on the next section. The authors have reviewed their main themes on a summary review board at the end of each section.

There are also a few suggestions for further reading at the end of each section.

REFERENCES

Education Reform Act (1988) HMSO.

Care Sector Consortium (1991) *National Occupational Standards for working with young children and their families.* Available from National Children's Bureau.

Department of Education and Science (1990) *Starting with Quality: Report of the Committee of Inquiry into the Educational Experiences offered to three and four-year-olds (Rumbold Report).* HMSO, London.

Pugh, G. (ed) (1992) *Contemporary Issues in the Early Years: Working collaboratively for children.* Paul Chapman Publishing.

Making Assessment Work

BEING A GROUP LEADER

INTRODUCTION TO THE SECTION

The role of the group leader is crucial to how this pack is used. The purpose of the pack is to encourage participants to think about what, how, when and why they assess children's learning rather than identify instant fool-proof answers, and so the group leader's role is not to instruct but to enable the group to participate, to think, to draw on their own experiences, to reflect and to learn.

Using the activities in this pack assumes some preliminary training or experience on the part of the group leader, particularly in equal opportunities training.

This section will probably be most useful for people who have had some experience of leading groups, or of working in groups, in the past, and would like some support and reassurance before going on to use the pack with a group of early years educators. It has been written for use by a small group of such people, who might well be colleagues from one early years setting who have decided to share out between themselves the duties and responsibilities of being a group leader. If it is not possible to establish such a group it would be worth finding at least one other person to work with on the activities that follow: they are based on the principles of trust, respect and mutual support, which are the corner-stones of effective work in groups, for both group leaders and group members.

In this section, we have tried to acknowledge the expertise and understanding that group leaders will bring to their work, and to admit openly that being a group leader can sometimes be a demanding, stressful, even unhappy, experience.

We have also tried to recognise that all group leaders, whatever their previous experience, have set out on a journey of learning, a journey that, however rewarding, is sometimes also hard going. Keeping one's eye on the concept of learning, as one works at 'being a group leader' may help to make the experience more worthwhile.

The purposes of this section are:

* to offer group leaders some practical suggestions for effective group work

* to offer support in the emotional and personal challenges of leading a group

The section opens with some general notes for group leaders, based on those in our earlier pack **Working with Children: developing a curriculum for the early years** (Drummond, Lally, Pugh 1989). These notes are followed by four activities and we would recommend that you do them all. If you are not part of a group, then it is worth doing them on your own and, if possible, discussing them with a colleague.

Making Assessment Work

The value of group work

There are many advantages of working in groups, the greatest of which is the opportunity it provides for *learning from and building on our own experiences*.

The group may act to:

- *support active learning* by providing opportunities to learn from each other through tackling problems and tasks cooperatively

- *reveal hidden strengths* and potential in individuals, where helping and leadership come from members of the group

- *provide a sounding board* where other people are on hand to listen to ideas and offer a range of responses and give opinions

- *give emotional support* by helping people to value their own ideas and experiences and by alleviating feelings of isolation

- *recognise that most people have worries* and feelings of inadequacy, and to share ways of overcoming or coping with them

- *promote participation* with openness in the group acting as a model for working more closely with colleagues in the workplace and with parents

However, working in groups can be difficult and there are a number of areas to be careful about and pitfalls to avoid.

- *Careful planning* is needed to ensure the group tackles the work effectively. Having co-leaders can provide support and help.

- *People's expectations* and perceptions of groups are often very different. It is important to clarify the aims of the group at the beginning to diminish the possibility of anger or disappointment. A short workshop series may not be able to meet all expectations, but a longer series of events could be planned later by the group?

- *People's confidence* and ability to participate in groups vary. Some people speak a great deal and others are often silent. All need to be respected.

- *Some groups can become destructive* with highly critical and judgemental atmosphere. Focusing on the materials and encouraging constructive criticism and positive comments will help groups work effectively together.

- *An agreement on confidentiality* should be established within the group before asking for personal sharing amongst members.

- *Splitting people into pairs and small groups* makes it easier for some to participate in the discussion. Clear instructions on what should be reported back to the large group are important, so that key points of discussion are not lost, while individual confidences are respected.

Making Assessment Work

The group leader's task is to enable group members to think and learn, rather than to impart information or to instruct.

This will mean:

- *planning the course* as a whole as well as each individual session

- *relating each session*, and the material presented for discussion, to the experience and the needs of group members. You may want to add to or change the examples on the handouts to support and challenge your group

- *reviewing and evaluating* each session before planning the next

- *facilitating learning*, through listening, encouraging, probing, and consolidating

- *building* on the expertise and experience that members bring to the group

- *challenging* group members to look critically at what they do with young children: this will include challenging racist and discriminatory attitudes and promoting attention to equal opportunities for all children

- *using questions* to help group members to reflect on their assumptions and expectations - rather than 'teaching' your own view, or offering your own experiences or knowledge

- *clarifying issues* in the group and drawing together the points made in discussion. The review at the end of each section will support you in this. It will also be an opportunity for you to state your own beliefs, refer to relevant research, and suggest further reading

CO-LEADERSHIP

Some people find running groups easier if they work as a pair of co-leaders. It can be very supportive to have someone else to plan sessions with and to review what is happening. Two leaders also offer the opportunity for group members to relate to two different personalities and leadership styles.

Co-leadership is an excellent way of training new group leaders: an apprenticeship model for someone who has participated in groups and understands the mechanics, but needs some support and experience in group leadership.

If co-leadership is chosen, it is important that both people are clear about who is doing what: leading group exercises and activities, chairing open discussion groups or plenary sessions, taking notes. All these tasks can be successfully shared, provided that both people concerned are clear about who is doing what.

BEING A GROUP LEADER

Making Assessment Work

BEING A GROUP LEADER

Organising sessions

BEFORE THE GROUP MEETINGS BEGIN:

- *Who* is coming? Who will invite or inform them? What is the best size for this group?

- *What* will the overall format of events or activities be? How many, how often and how long will the group meetings be? How much will it cost? How will it be funded?

- *Where* will the group meet?

- *When* will it meet?

- *How* will the time be organised? Do these events have to fit into a previously structured programme/a staff meeting/a lunch hour?

- *Who* will be involved in making all these decisions? How will the information be made available to others?

The size of the group will be determined by a number of different factors, not least the size of the room(s) available. The materials in this pack have been designed primarily for use in pairs and small groups of up to 12 people, who may form part of a much larger group.

It is difficult to have large group discussions with more than 20 people. If you are planning a one day seminar for 60-70 people, several experienced leaders will be necessary to allow you to break into small work groups.

ON ARRIVAL

Who will be responsible for:

- welcoming group members?
- refreshments?
- setting up the furniture/equipment?
- starting off the group meeting?

STARTING OFF

Even when members of a group already know each other, it is important to start the first meeting in a way that is active, welcoming, inclusive of all, and that demonstrates the participatory and sharing nature of the group.

One way is to ask each group member to talk to his or her neighbour for four to five minutes and then to introduce each other to the group. If there is to be a series of meetings, the first one should be primarily given over to clarifying the purpose and aims of the group, negotiating an agreed programme, establishing ground rules and identifying what individual members have to offer the group.

THE MAIN ACTIVITIES

In planning which activities to include, it is important, not only to have a clear focus for the session, but also to be prepared to respond to the contributions made by members of the group. Their experience and concerns may mean you have to work more slowly - or more quickly - or re-plan your next session.

If the session is being planned as part of a longer course, or if the group members come from a variety of workplaces, the group leader should act as a resource and a facilitator, rather than participating in the individual exercises. You will need to observe and listen to group members' response to the activities to enable you to tune into their concerns and to help you to match the content of future sessions to the group's needs. However if you are running a session (or series of sessions) within your own workplace with your colleagues, it is important that you take part in the activities and share your experience with the rest of the group.

Making Assessment Work

Organising sessions

ESTABLISHING RULES

It is important to negotiate with the group and establish some working rules before you start. You will want to consider:

- *group membership:* is it an open group with a fluctuating membership, or a closed group of named people only? Are they committed to attend every meeting?

- *how to emphasise a positive and constructive approach:* encourage any critical feedback to include an alternative way of behaving

- *using the group to learn from:* while nobody should feel forced to take part in any of the activities, group members should be encouraged to take personal responsibility for their learning and to use the group to explore new ways of thinking

- *expectations:* how will individual expectations be negotiated if they are inconsistent with the group goals and resources?

- *confidentiality:* all information shared between individuals within the group should be treated as confidential

- *time-keeping:* start on time, end on time and agree the use of time between and within group meetings

KEEPING THE GROUP 'ON TASK'

The group leader needs to be able to draw on group members' experience but also to keep the group focused on the task. This will mean, amongst other things:

- moving the group on to the next part of the task at the appropriate time to ensure that all parts of the task are tackled. The group may not need to 'finish' every part of every task

- helping to keep contributions relevant. This may require intervention; for example, when a group member has launched into a lengthy, irrelevant anecdote, by saying 'I'm sorry to interrupt you, but I'm not sure that's exactly what we're looking for at the moment. Time is running by, and we need to have completed this by .... so I'm afraid I'll have to stop you'...

- recording group members' contributions with notes or on the flip chart or large piece of paper provided, so everyone is clear about what they have achieved so far.

FINISHING THE SESSIONS AND THE COURSE

There are two parts to finishing a group or series of meetings: evaluating what has happened, and looking ahead to the future.

Evaluation involves considering:

- what has been learnt by individual members of the group?
- has the group achieved its goals?
- how did the activities help achieve those goals?
- what helped, hindered, challenged group members?
- what else could the group have done?
- what was missing?

Looking ahead involves considering:

- does the group plan to meet again?
- if so, when, why, how?

It is important to take time at the end of every session to reflect with the group members on what they have been doing, what they have learned, and difficulties they have experienced.

After a few sessions, group members will probably be secure enough to express their feelings about the course. This can be a valuable source of feedback for individuals, for the group and for the group leaders.

**Activity 1
Learning in
groups**

INTRODUCTION TO THE ACTIVITY

In this activity you will be able to think back over your own experiences, and reflect on what you already know about being a member and, possibly, a leader of a group.

The purpose of the activity is to help you to

- identify some of the characteristics of working with other adults that can help make group discussions challenging and worthwhile;

- reflect on the contributions that you have made and will make to group work with adults.

Working on your own, think back to a time when you were a member, or possibly a leader, of a group of adults who seemed to work really well together. It might be a group that has nothing to do with your work with young children. Perhaps you once belonged to a hang-gliding club or a wholefood collective? Try to remember some of the reasons why the group worked so well, and jot them down on a sheet of paper. Be as specific and detailed as you can. Talk over what you have written with one other person, noting any similarities and especially any differences in your experiences. Try to think about the reasons for these. Think about your personal contribution to the groups you are describing: what part did you play in making them effective? Encourage each other to blow your own trumpet for once in a while!

Now work with a partner to think about what contribution the group leader(s) made to the positive experiences you've been remembering. You may also find yourself remembering some groups where you had a more difficult time; try to use these memories to help you list some of the things that effective leaders do, and don't do. (For example, 'She always finished on time.' 'He never interrupted me, even when I found it difficult to express myself - not like old so and so ...')

Work in two groups to build on your discussion so far by making two lists. One group will list their expectations of group leaders from the point of view of group **members.** The other group will list their expectations of **themselves** as group leaders. Write the lists on large sheets so you can share them later.

Get together to compare lists, and to think about what they mean for your work. Do the lists describe wonder-woman and superman, robots, or ordinary human beings like yourselves?

Bring this discussion to a close with a few comments of your own, looking back over all the lists and notes you've made during the activity. Think about the ways in which you feel you can contribute to the kind of group work you've been discussing. Remember, there is no such person as the perfect group leader. Being 'good enough' is enough to aim for, and learning to be good enough is one of the things you will be working on throughout the pack.

**Activity 2
But what if?**

BEING A GROUP LEADER

INTRODUCTION TO THE ACTIVITY

You ended the last discussion on a positive note, thinking about the contributions you have made, and will continue to make, to effective group work. Now you will have the opportunity to think about some of the less appealing aspects of being a group leader.

It is important not to miss out this activity, either to save time or because you are not working as part of a group. Do it on your own if necessary, but then try to find a colleague to discuss it with.

The purpose of this activity is for you to:

* discuss strategies to draw on as a group leader when the group becomes difficult to work with

* identify some general principles about work with adults.

You will need the list of 'BUT WHAT IF' incomplete sentences on page 25.

*Making
Assessment
Work*

Working on your own, complete the sentences on the 'BUT WHAT IF ...?' sheet (p25).

Talk about what you have written with one other person, concentrating on the sentences that describe your feelings. It will be interesting to see whether your partner's feelings of anxiety - or guilt - or even panic - are triggered by the same sorts of events as yours. ·Or perhaps your partner doesn't turn a hair at some of the things that keep you awake at night - or vice versa. The differences between you may help you to understand and accept your own feelings.

Now work in a larger group if possible (of four or five people) to talk about the possible responses you might make as group leader to each of the problems you have discussed. Be sure to hear from each member of the group, so that you really do have a range of responses to consider and evaluate. Think carefully about whether you feel you could learn from other people's suggestions.

It's hard to generalise about the problems and difficulties of group work, because they are often so specific: they may seem to be caused by a particular person in the group, or by the specially controversial topic you are working on, or by the uncomfortable room you are working in. But there are some strategies that can be effective at almost any difficult moment. Work with one other person to talk about the three different approaches described below. How useful would each of these be for you?

- 'Whenever I find myself in a sticky position I think about my experience of working with Diana, who was a fantastic group leader. I think to myself: what would she have done? What would she say now? Then I try to re-interpret her words - and actions - so that I can make them my own - as well as keeping the spirit of her approach.'

- 'I often found myself not knowing quite what to do when I was leading the group, but luckily I had a good friend who was working with a similar group, using the same materials, so before - and after - each meeting, we'd talk through any dodgy bits and give each other lots of good ideas - and plenty of reassurance too. Especially after the meetings - our phone bills were colossal!'

- 'Difficult moments? Oh don't remind me! I used to freeze like a rabbit. But then I hit on the idea of telling the group how I felt, and getting them to help me out. I'd say something like, "I really don't know how to handle this right now - has anyone got a suggestion for what we should do to sort this out?", and then the problem didn't feel so overwhelming. It was as if we could all share responsibility for what was happening. I didn't feel so isolated, as if everything depended on **me!**'

Making

Assessment

Work

BEING A GROUP LEADER

Activity 2
But what if?

In your discussions so far, you've been reviewing and evaluating different strategies you might draw on as a group leader when the going gets a little tough. Your choice of the most appropriate strategy will be the result of many factors - but underlying your choice will be some general principles about working with adults.

Work on your own for a few minutes to look at the list of 'principles of procedure' given below. Can you prioritise them in order of importance to you? Try to pick out the three most essential, the ones that you would never want to lose sight of, whatever else happened.

PRINCIPLES OF PROCEDURE

- The principle that everyone in the group has the right to be treated with respect.

- The principle that everyone has the right to speak and the right to be silent.

- The principle of trying to understand what each person says, even if I don't agree with it.

- The principle of challenging a statement that I find unacceptable

- The principle of accepting other people's negative feelings and encouraging them to express them

- The principle of accepting my own negative feelings - and sometimes expressing them

- The principle of sticking to our own working rules.

- The principle of tender loving care....

You will want to add some more of your own.

Work with one other person to discuss the priorities you have marked on the list above. Think about the reasons for the choices you have made.

End this discussion by telling everyone in the group the principle that you hold to most firmly - the one that you'd go to the stake for.

Making Assessment Work

BEING A GROUP LEADER

My worst fears about running a group are...

....

I will know the group is having problems when ....

....

My response as a group leader may be ....

....

When someone in the group confronts me, I feel ....

....

My response as a group leader may be ....

....

When someone in the group interrupts me, I feel ....

....

My response as a group leader may be ....

....

When someone in the group looks distracted and bored, I feel..............................

....

My response as a group leader may be ....

....

When someone in the group becomes depressed and tearful, I feel.......................

....

My response as a group leader may be ....

....

When someone seems to be convinced that s/he knows all the answers, I feel ....

....

My response as a group leader may be ....

....

**Activity 3
Taking care**

INTRODUCTION TO THE ACTIVITY

One evening I was moaning about feeling tired and neglected .... 'I want my Mum.' My friend Carrie stopped me. 'Oh no you don't. You know quite well what your mother would say: "You've been working too hard, you've been burning the candle at both ends, you're not eating properly, you've only yourself to blame ..." That's not what you want. You want someone to take care of you, **without** all of that. And here's the supper.'

She was right. When we feel the need of someone to take care of us, it isn't every kind of care that fits the bill. Sometimes people's helpfulness can make us feel worse. Sometimes people's good intentions don't work out as they meant them to.

The purpose of this activity is for you to:

* think about how adults can take care of each other as they work together, without unintentionally hurting each other

You will need your list of PRINCIPLES OF PROCEDURE from the last activity.

Spend a few minutes on your own thinking about an occasion when someone's well meant support had the opposite effect on you.

She came in and washed all my paint pots. I felt humiliated

She corrected a letter I'd written .... I felt furious!

Talk about the whole incident with one other person. Try to see it from the helpful person's point of view, but don't lose sight of your own aggrieved feelings, which were very real to you at the time.

Look back at the list of principles you worked on in the last activity. Do any of these help you see how people 'taking care' can avoid hurting other people's feelings?

Think about a time when you felt very much in need of someone to take care of you. Without going into all the details of why you were feeling that way, talk with one other person about the kinds of things you'd have liked to hear from a caring person. Try and list some of the caring things they might say. For example:

- do you want to talk about it?
- do you want to be left alone?
- what would you like me to do?
- shall I look after the dinner session today?
- shall we get together this evening for a talk?

When there are eight or nine questions or comments on your list, work with your partner to think about how these approaches could be used in your work as group leader. What are the equivalents of these expressions in small group discussion work? What are the resources within a group that we can all draw on in taking care of each other?

Would you like me to supervise the felt tip pens today?

Making Assessment Work

Activity 3
Taking Care

Read the following extract from the poem **The Galloping Cat** by Stevie Smith. Would you like to work in a discussion group with the galloping cat? Or would you prefer to work with David Smail, the author of the paragraph quoted below.

THE GALLOPING CAT

Oh I am a cat that likes to
Gallop about doing good
So
One day when I was
Galloping about doing good, I saw
A Figure in the path; I said;
Get off! (Because
I am a cat that likes to
Gallop about doing good)
But he did not move, instead
He raised his hand as if
To land me a cuff
So I made to dodge so as to
Prevent him bringing it orf ....
.... So
His hand caught me on the cheek
I tried
To lay his arm open from wrist to elbow
With my sharp teeth
Because I am
A cat that likes to gallop about doing good
Would you believe it?
He wasn't there
My teeth met nothing but air ....

Stevie Smith (1972) *Scorpion and other poems* Longman.

'We would do better to see ourselves as plants rather than as machines, and we might benefit from applying to our own lives some very elementary rules of horticulture .... Plants grow best in well understood and carefully prepared conditions - of sun or shade, damp or dryness, heat or cold, in this or that kind of soil .... It does seem strange to me that we should often lavish so much more attention on our gardens than on our fellow beings. Nobody expects their cauliflowers to grow by magic .... Given a safe enough environment, it seems to me that most people are glad of an opportunity to love their fellows.'

David Smail (1987)*Taking Care - an alternative to therapy* p92 and 101 Dent

Making
Assessment
Work

INTRODUCTION TO THE ACTIVITY

Your own style as a group leader will evolve gradually, in the course of your work, and you will be influenced by other group leaders you have worked with. But it may also be helpful to think about some of the different strategies for achieving effective communication suggested by various writers. There is a wealth of published material on the subject and you will want to evaluate this material carefully, to see what is helpful for you.

The purpose of this activity is for you to:

* consider different approaches to leading a group and different styles of communication

Working on your own, spend a few minutes reflecting on this list of words and phrases that are sometimes used to describe the things that group leaders do.

responsive listening	being consistent
reflective listening	being congruent
facilitating	nurturing
valuing individuals	controlling
reciprocal exchange	adapting
the dance of rapport	non-verbal communication
confronting	directing
challenging	meeting the needs of the group

Discuss with a partner what these words really mean.

Do they describe your talk, your behaviour?

What do you actually do, and think, and feel, and say, when you are being a group leader?

**Activity 4
Making
choices**

Now read the extracts that follow (pp31-33).

'SILENCE, OBSERVATION, UNDERSTANDING AND LISTENING' describes an approach to working with children that is part of the High/Scope curriculum

'COMMUNICATION SKILLS' gives a selection of material developed by Parent Network.

Working with a partner, think about these questions:

- What do these ideas mean to you?

- Have you used strategies like these in discussion groups in the past?

- How do each of these strategies match the principles that you thought about in the discussion 'But What If ....?'

- Do any of these strategies cross over the dangerous border-line between being effective and being manipulative?

- Which of these communication strategies might you choose?

- What do you think? What do you feel? Would you like to know more? (If so, see the list of references at the end of this section).

SILENCE, OBSERVATION, UNDERSTANDING AND LISTENING (S.O.U.L.)

Approaching an interaction with children using the steps of silence, observation, understanding and listening (SOUL), reduces the chance that you will interrupt children's play. In order to communicate with children successfully it is important that you become partners in their endeavours. Using the technique of SOUL means that you allow the children to initiate, that you spend more time observing, that you become more sensitive to their different needs, and that you become an effective listener - all techniques designed to allow you to enter their play and so communicate effectively with them.

Glossary of Communication Strategies

Self talk

Here the adult is labelling what s/he is doing, describing and demonstrating and talking in the context of an activity. For example, 'I am getting the bowl and spoon out of the cupboard ready to make a cake'.

Parallel talk

In parallel talk, you describe what the child is doing. As you interact with the child you comment on where the child is playing, what the child is playing with, and possibly what the child is doing.

Repeat

After listening carefully to a child, you repeat what the child has said. Repeating is effective because it clarifies what the child has said, serves as an acknowledgement, is very supportive of the language/words the child uses, and often keeps children talking because it acts like a question and indicates that you're interested in what they have to say.

Restate

Sometimes children make mistakes when communicating. When a child makes a language error, you can repeat what they said in the correct form without drawing attention to the error. You are modelling correct language in a positive, non-punitive manner that facilitates communication.

Expanding

In natural conversation, the adult often adds new ideas to what the children are saying. For example:

Child: 'That pigeon is flying up high.'
Adult: 'Yes, the pigeon is as high as the tree, but the aeroplane can fly even higher.'

Encouraging ideas

Encourage children to articulate their solutions and ideas by asking them how they solved something; by describing what they will do and what they did; and by asking them to help you. The last strategy is particularly valuable because it indicates your respect for their ideas and solutions to problems.

Open-ended questions

Questions that have more than one right answer, or ones that can be answered in many ways are called 'open-ended' or 'divergent' questions. These questions stimulate more language, respect the diversity of solutions, affirm children's ideas, and encourage creative thinking.

From: High/Scope (1986) *Introduction to the High/Scope Pre-School Curriculum.* A two-day workshop High/Scope Education Research Foundation, Ypsilanti, Michigan.

Do you think these techniques, developed for working with children, could also be useful in working with groups of adults?

*Making
Assessment
Work*

**Activity 4
Making
choices**

COMMUNICATION SKILLS

Reflective listening

Reflective listening is the skill of mirroring back to a person, in our own words and manner, what that person is saying to us.

Reflective listening allows the speakers to hear what they are saying, see what they are meaning and feel what is happening and, through this process, come to a better understanding of themselves and their issues.

At its simplest level, it is a process of listening with full attention, and includes paraphrasing what the speaker says.

Paraphrasing what the other has said also goes a long way towards preventing misunderstanding - we often think or feel that we understand what a person has said but this may just be guesswork unless we check our understanding out with the speaker.

Consistency and congruency

Our response to behaviour is not naturally consistent. Part of being human is that we change our minds frequently about what we think, believe and feel. Being consistent about how we deal with behaviour imposes unnatural limits on our responses to the world and prevents us from living life as it is.

Trying to deal consistently with the same behaviour in different adults can also lead to problems. Just as we are unique individuals, so are the group members, and trying to treat them as if they were all the same is not useful for us or them.

We are not asking you to display no consistency at all, just suggesting that it is more useful to be consistent in the realms of honesty, openness and love. If you are consistently honest with group members about what you want and what you feel, they will respect and trust you, and are far more likely to be honest themselves.

Being congruent means that all the different parts of you match. They are all expressing the same thing.

For example, if we are angry, we would look and sound angry, we would be thinking angry thoughts and we would be expressing ourselves verbally in an angry way.

*Making
Assessment
Work*

Being congruent involves being aware of our experiences, knowing what we are feeling and thinking and being able to communicate these things to others.

Being a facilitator, valuing individuals

A facilitator is someone who has the role of helping participants learn in an experimental group.

If as facilitators we believe that we value individuals taking responsibility and decisions about their learning, then our actions while leading the groups will need to reflect this.

Acceptance

Being able to accept each individual as having feelings of his or her own we may not like; thoughts and ideas we may not approve of - being able to say to ourselves, 'I may not like what is happening with this person and yet I can accept that it is happening and try and help her help herself in finding a way forward'.

Care

Even as we are able to accept individuals and what is happening for them, we need to be able genuinely to care about them enough to be able to want to help them, both now with their learning and in the long term, by helping them take responsibility for their future learning.

Understanding

Sometimes it is hard for us as group leaders to make sense of what those in our groups are going through. Part of being a facilitator is taking the time to think ourselves into someone else's shoes - 'What might she be feeling like right now' not in order to present her with our ready-made solutions but to be able to work alongside her in her task to find her own.

Trust

None of the above is any use if we do not believe that other people are actually capable of understanding their own feelings and issues, finding their own answers and looking after their own interests. We need to be able to trust them to develop responsibility for their own learning, including, perhaps, asking us for assistance along the way. As we trust them more, they will come to trust themselves more and will grow - learning from their mistakes along the way - to be more and more capable.

Nimet Rener, from work with Parent Network (see Sokolov and Hutton 1988).

*Making
Assessment
Work*

BEING A GROUP LEADER

Postscript

POSTSCRIPT

Throughout this pack, which has been written for use in small groups of committed and collaborative adults, we are advocating a particular set of relationships, both between group members, and between group members and group leaders. We believe in the need for relationships that are secure but not cosy, in which we can challenge each other without destroying each other, in which we can feel safe enough to take risks, in which we can take care without molly-coddling each other. This state of affairs has been vividly described by Roger Harrison (1962), an American expert and consultant in management. He writes:

> 'We cannot increase learning by destroying the defences which block it. What we can do is create situations where people will not need to stay behind their defences all the time. We can make it safe to sally forth from behind the moat, so to speak, secure in the knowledge that while we are exploring the countryside no-one will sneak in and burn the castle.'

Maybe this will be a useful idea to think back to from time to time during your work on this pack.

REFERENCES

Drummond, M. J., Lally, M., and Pugh, G. (1989) *Working with Children: developing a curriculum in the early years.* NES Arnold and the National Children's Bureau.

Harrison, R. (1962) 'Defences and the need to know' in *Human Relations Training News.* 6, (Winter 1962-63), pp 266-272.

High/Scope (1966) *Introduction to the High/Scope Pre-School Curriculum.* High/Scope Educational Research Foundation. Ypsilanti, Michigan.

Sokolov, I. and Hutton, D. (1988) *The Parents' Book* Thorsons Publishing Group.

Making Assessment Work

SECTION 1

Looking at values

1

INTRODUCTION

The purpose of this section is to help you think about the part that educators' values play in the assessment of young children. Later sections of the pack will examine the things that adults actually do in their assessment practice. But here you will have the opportunity to look at some of the ways in which you think and behave in your everyday life, when you are not doing anything that could be labelled assessment. You will be able to see the connections between the person you are and the judgements you make.

When we look at some things in the world, we see what anyone would see. But when we look at children it isn't so simple. Look at this baby and think about what you see.

I see a baby being comforted

All I can see is a baby with a dummy

I see a neglected child - where's the mother?

I see a child who is being spoiled

I see a child whose language development is being harmed

When we look at children, and interact with them, we interpret and make meaning of what we see, even if we aren't aware of what we're doing. The assessments we make of children will be affected by the interpretations we make of our observations. Our interpretations are affected by our values and beliefs. So we need to be aware of these values, and able to talk about them and explain them. We will never be able to make completely neutral observations, but we can learn to be more aware of the values that underlie our observations and assessments. We can learn to understand more about what we **expect** children to do, to think, to feel and to be. We can learn to see how these expectations affect the ways in which we respond to what children **actually** do and think and feel.

Our attitudes, beliefs and values have been forming from our own childhoods onwards. When we are looking after and working with other people's children, we have to be able to recognise and explore these values, which we hold very deeply. We feel very strongly about how we should care for and educate children. It isn't necessarily a pleasant experience to have these feelings questioned and challenged. It isn't easy to be asked to look deeply inside ourselves, at our dearly-held beliefs, which seem to us so natural and inevitable.

And so the work on this section of the pack will sometimes be difficult, sometimes challenging, sometimes painful. But the exploration of our values and beliefs will have been worthwhile if it helps us learn more about how and why we see what we see, and do what we do, in our work with young children.

The purposes of this section are for you to:

- look inside yourself, at your basic assumptions, values and beliefs about children and childhood

- think about how your professional training, and your personal experiences of childhood, have affected the ways in which you interact with and understand children

- come to understand more about the connection between your values and beliefs, and what you do, say and think in your work with young children

There are eight activities in this section, from which you will want to choose four or five, including the first and the last. Later in your work on the pack you may want to return to the activities you have not used; but it is essential to do some of the activities from this section before moving on to later sections of the pack.

ACTIVITY 1A   Ages and stages

PREPARATION

Pens and notebooks
Copies of the Handout, or a selection of examples from this Handout, with some added examples of your own, appropriate for your group members.

about 1 hour

Notes to Group Leaders

If you are working with a staff group it may be best for working partners to work together. In a mixed group it may be preferable for people from different settings and disciplines to pair up, so that they have a chance to extend their experience, share their expertise, and begin to question each other's assumptions and prejudices.

As this is the first discussion activity of the pack, it is very important for group members to feel able to talk freely and openly about their family and professional experiences. You will already have made an agreement about confidentiality with the group, and members will welcome the reassurance that this gives them.

As group members work on theHandout **Ages and stages**, they may be tempted to avoid the real issues with comments like: 'It all depends ....' and 'Whenever they are ready ....' You may need to help these group members take their thinking a little further with some (gentle) challenging comments. You might ask if they would expect to see a child breast feeding at five, or using a sharp tool at two .... and so on.

INTRODUCTION TO THE ACTIVITY

The purposes of this activity are for you to think about:

* the ways in which you use children's age as a measure of the things they say and do

* whether using children's age is an appropriate way of making judgements about their learning and development

*Making
Assessment
Work*

| ACTIVITY 1A | Ages and stages |

1. When Elizabeth Barrett Browning was forty-years-old, her maid Wilson was taken ill. So for the first time in her life, Elizabeth had to dress herself and brush her own hair. Later she made her maid some toast. She was very proud of doing this - another first!

   Working in pairs, think about the ages when you think that children should be able to do the things listed on the Handout. Don't be tempted to dodge the issues with comments like .... 'it all depends ....' or '.... when they are ready ....' Imagine your feelings (surprise? shock?) if you met a grown woman of forty who had never learned to brush her own hair - or use scissors - or boil a kettle ....

2. Work with another pair to compare your responses to the Handout, noting the agreements and disagreements between you, especially the disagreements.

3. Come together as a whole group to identify the items on the list that gave rise to most discussion. Think about **why** this might be. **Why** do opinions differ on this topic? **Why** do you think as you do?

4. Consider whether your views on '**Ages and stages**' are different in different contexts.
   - For boys and girls?
   - For children with different cultural heritages?
   - For children with physical disabilities?
   - For children with special learning needs?
   - For your own children, or children who are special to you?

   Think about **why** there might be differences in your views.

5. Bring the discussion to a close by thinking about some occasions in your workplace when you wanted to know the age of a child.
   - Why did you need to know?
   - What did you do with the information?
   - What difference did it make to your thinking? Your actions? Your judgements?

   Work together to consider when it **is** really important to know how old children are, and when it is **not** a significant factor in helping you understand their learning and development.

*Making
Assessment
Work*

HANDOUT 1A   Ages and stages

Please use a selection of the items on this list, adding more of your own that are appropriate for you and your group members.

I THINK THE AGE WHEN CHILDREN SHOULD...

But we just haven't got the facilities to change nappies in our Family Room

My Danish cousin didn't even go to school till he was 7

We had a terrible accident with a saw once

come out of nappies is ...
learn to read ...
look at picture books ...
use scissors/a saw/a glue gun...
know the names of colours...
use colours accurately to represent skin, hair and so on in drawings and models...
boil a kettle and make a hot drink...
own a penknife...
count to ten...
wait patiently for their turn...
say please and thank you...
put away their own toys...
....
....
....

You should see my husband in the supermarket queue

We don't even have words for please and thank you in my home language

Making Assessment Work

about 30 minutes

PREPARATION

Copies of the Handout
The set of pictures of children provided on pp 1.7-1.11 to be displayed where everyone can see them.
Any additional pictures provided by the group leader to challenge assumptions

Notes to Group Leaders

You may wish to reassure group members that this is not an exercise in finding the 'right' words to describe the pictures provided. It is an opportunity to look at the differences between the members' first impressions of a set of pictures that have been carefully chosen to trigger a range of different responses. Some responses may cause surprise, or amusement; you will be able to help group members share their feelings about each other's unexpected descriptions, to listen carefully, and to consider another person's point of view.

However, some responses may be unacceptable to you and other group members. Responses that express a stereotype, a prejudice, or racist or sexist attitudes will need to be challenged. These responses will make an important contribution to the group's discussion, but only if they are identified, challenged and openly discussed. If you are anxious about this, you might consider talking it over with a colleague, or another group leader, rehearsing the kinds of responses you might make. You could also look back at the activity 'But what if...?' in **Being a group leader.**

INTRODUCTION TO THE ACTIVITY

All the people we have ever met, all the places we have visited, all the things we have seen and heard, have left impressions on us. Our experiences of the world and the people in it have shaped our attitudes and our values: these in turn affect our judgements and our interpretations of the world.

In this activity you will use a set of pictures of young children to help you think about:

- how your previous experience, your attitudes, your values, consciously or unconsciously, affect your responses to these pictures

- how other group members respond to the same set of pictures

- why there are differences in people's perceptions of children

- how differences in perception affect your observations and assessment of young children

Making Assessment Work

© John Birdsall Photography

Posed by model

Picture courtesy of 'Mamas & Papas'

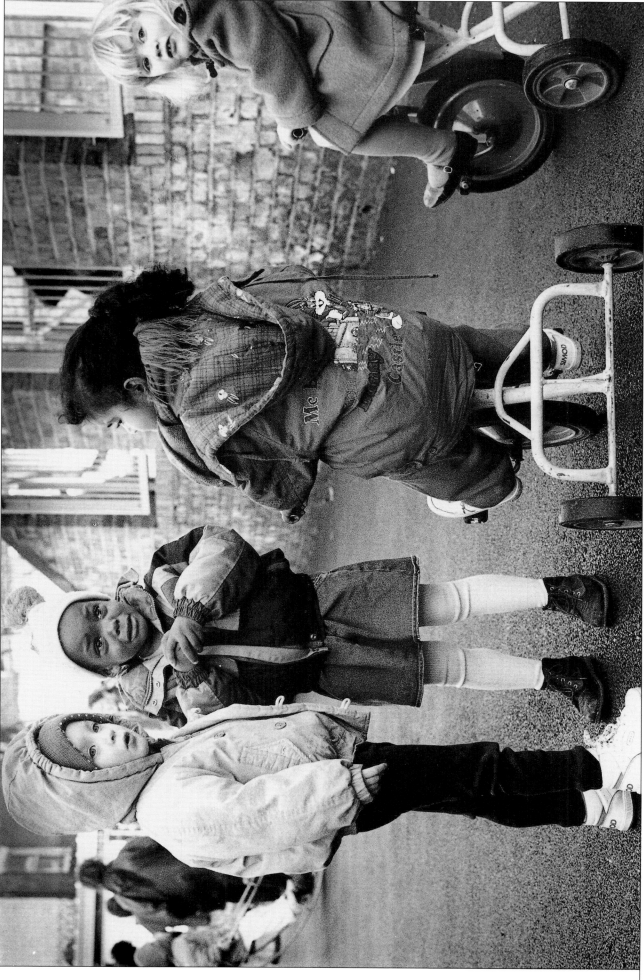

© Sara Hannant

Posed by models

1. Working alone, look at the pictures of children provided, which have been chosen to give you a range of different impressions.
    On the Handout provided, jot down a descriptive word or phrase for each picture. At this stage don't give your most carefully thought-out professional opinion - just note down your first impression - your gut reaction - which you'll be able to qualify and reflect on later in the activity.

2. Work with one other person to share your first impressions, noting the similarities and differences in your responses. Think about the reasons why you agree or disagree over particular pictures, and about some of the influences that have shaped your attitudes. For example: your parents? grandparents? parents-in-law? What would they say about these pictures?

3. In the whole group, reflect on what you have noticed so far about the ways in which different people responded. Listen carefully to other group members' responses, trying to see their points of view. However, if you consider their interpretations to be prejudiced or stereotyped, you will want to challenge what they say. Racist and sexist responses too must be identified and discussed.

4. In the discussion so far, you and your colleagues have talked about some of your experiences, your attitudes and your values. Conclude the discussion by thinking about the connection between this - often unspoken - value system and your work with children. How do your values and beliefs affect:

    •   your observations of children?

    •   your interactions with children?

    •   your passing comments to your colleagues?

    •   your judgements about children's learning and development?

HANDOUT 1B **People like us?**

I see a child who

1. ....
....
....
....

2. ....
....
....

3. ....
....
....

4. ....
....
....

5. ....
....
....

I don't know **why** I feel this - but I do!

I probably shouldn't – but …

Oh!

That's me!

My mum would go mad.

I always wanted to...

People do say...

That's not fair.

delicious!

Just like my Sam

I know what my Granny would say

Perhaps if we all...

How sad...

I have heard that...

My brother...

I wish it was me !

you lucky beggar !

dodgy...

Good Heavens!

Whatever Next?

Making Assessment Work

about 45 minutes
to an hour

| ACTIVITY 1C | Not till you're older |

PREPARATION

Pens and notebooks

Notes to Group Leaders

In this activity, group members are asked to share personal memories about their childhood and their families. Your agreement on confidentiality will help people feel free to talk about things they remember that may still evoke painful or angry feelings. Individual group members may need time to talk about some of the occasions when they felt thwarted or dominated by the powerful adults in their lives.

Most of the work in this activity will take place in small groups. You may want to draw the whole group together at the end, so that you can jointly reflect on the insights you have gained.

INTRODUCTION TO THE ACTIVITY

When you and your colleagues were little children, the adults who cared for you and educated you set limits on what you could and could not do.

In this activity you will be able to:

- think about how these early experiences of being controlled by adults did and do affect you

- think about the limits you now set on what children should and should not do

- discuss differences in approach between yourself and your colleagues

- consider how you and your colleagues respond to children who do not accept the limits you wish to impose

ACTIVITY 1C   Not till you're older

1.   Working alone, write down some of the things you remember on the left hand side of a sheet of paper headed

WHEN I WAS LITTLE I WASN'T ALLOWED TO

WHEN I WAS LITTLE I HAD TO ....

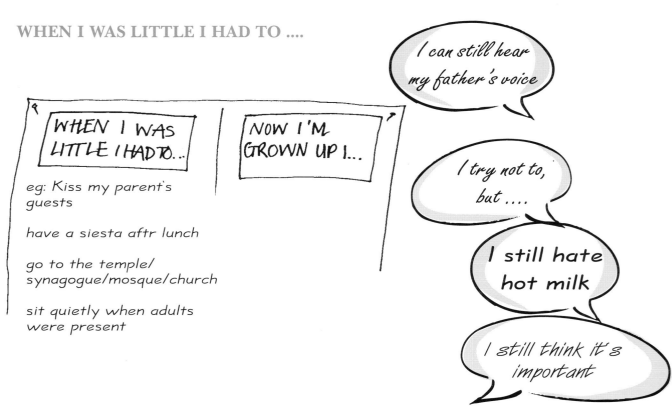

2.   Now write another column on the right-hand side, headed: BUT ACTUALLY I USED TO and NOW I'M GROWN-UP I...

Try to find examples that match what you have already written on the left-hand side.

Making Assessment Work

Whatever I did seemed to be wrong

I couldn't see the point. I thought they were silly

They kept saying I was a tomboy

I was very hurt

I learned not to get found out

3. Work with two or three other people, comparing and contrasting your experiences. Think about how you felt about these experiences, then .... and how you feel now.

Ask each other:

What did you learn from these limits on your behaviour?
*   about yourself?
*   about the adults around you?
*   about the conventions of society?

4. Now think about the connections between this discussion and your present work as educators of young children. Look at these questions on your own for a few minutes.

Do you now set similar limits and make similar rules to the ones imposed on you? Why?

Do you set different limits or different standards? Why?

How do the children respond? How do they feel? How do you know?

Talk about your responses to these questions with the same two or three people. Think about the differences and similarities between the children you once were and the children you work with now.

Do you ever think .... 'I used to feel like that when I was three .. or two .. or five? ..' Talk about when and why.

5. If you do recognise yourself - or parts of yourself - in the children you work with now, think about what effects this might have:

*   on what they do?
*   on what they want to do?
*   on what you ask them to do?
*   on what you make them do?
*   on what you allow them to do?
*   on what you prevent them from doing?

Making Assessment Work

ACTIVITY 1D   When I grow up

PREPARATION

Pens and notebooks
Flip chart sheets

about 45 minutes

Notes to Group Leaders

Some of the groups who worked on the trial version of this pack reported that they got involved in discussing what the children they worked with might really say about 'when they grew up.'

You may need to encourage group members to be more speculative, imagining the unimaginable, and then testing out their emotional reactions to it. Are the imaginary remarks acceptable or unacceptable? Why? You may need to maintain a steady pressure of questioning and probing.

The question about group members' own children (stage 3 of the activity) will almost certainly release some powerful reactions. You may need to reassure group members about your agreement on confidentiality.

INTRODUCTION TO THE ACTIVITY

In this activity you will be able to:

* think about some of your expectations for the future of the young children you work with

* consider the possibility that thinking about what might happen to children in later life may affect the ways in which you perceive them now.

*When I grow up I'm going to be a brain surgeon...
...or a ballet dancer..
..or a mermaid*

*Making
Assessment
Work*

1. Imagine you are eavesdropping while a group of young children are talking about growing up. Working in groups of four or five, think about what you would expect to hear, and what would really upset or startle you.

2. Working in the whole group, collect examples from each small group and write them on a flip chart, divided up like this:

> *I'd Expect To Hear....*
> fire fighter? nurse?
> housewife?
> astronaut?
> footballer?
> Wimbledon Champion
>
> *I'd Be Concerned To Hear....*
> tramp! millionaire!
> bull fighter?
> prostitute?,
> on the dole?
>   paki-basher?

Discuss your emotional responses to these imaginary children's aspirations.

Think about what these lists say about:
*   **your** aspirations for children
*   **your** values for children
*   **your** view of what they should or should not value or aspire to

3. Take the discussion a little further by thinking about whether it makes a difference who the children are who say these things.

    *   Does the gender of the child make a difference?
    *   Does the cultural heritage or ethnicity of the child make a difference?
    *   Would it make a difference if one of the children was your own daughter or son, or a child you are very close to?

4. Think back over the last few weeks and try to remember some occasions when you found yourself thinking about a child's future - in the next six months - in the next year - at school - at secondary school - as an adolescent - as an adult.
    *   Can you remember what triggered these thoughts?
    *   Does thinking about a child's future affect the clarity with which you can see the present?
    *   Does thinking about what might happen limit the possibilities for what can happen now?
    *   Does worrying about the future close off possibilities for what can happen now?

Making Assessment Work

Do your aspirations (for all children - and for particular individuals) affect the way you assess their learning and development?

ACTIVITY 1E	Toys from shops

PREPARATION

Copies of the two Handouts
Flipchart sheets
Pens and paper

BEFORE THE MEETING

If possible, collect examples of the kinds of toys listed on the
Handout and bring them to the meeting

at least an hour

Notes to Group Leaders

This activity is intended to start discussion about how some toys may encourage stereo-typical play activities and offer children unequal opportunities for learning and development. Your task will be to help to raise awareness of how educators' attitudes to certain kinds of play might affect their assessment practices, as well as children's learning.

For example, some group members may think that play with guns has positive outcomes, because it helps children to gain a sense of control, and to understand injury and death. These educators may consider children's play with guns as a worthwhile part of their development. However, some group members may think that playing with guns encourages children to behave aggressively and to act violently against people and property. Their assessments of this activity will be very different. You will be able to hold these different view-points up against one another and encourage group members to discuss the implications for their provision and practice.

You may also need to encourage some detailed consideration of HOW children play with particular toys. For example: is the play with guns about accidents, hospitals, medical treatment, predominantly about taking care of the wounded? Or is the focus of the play annihilation, pillage and plunder? Is the play a re-enactment of real experiences (for children from Northern Ireland, Beirut or Iraq) or is it an extension of adult fantasies from comics and television? Is a child's play with a gun an imitation of her father's target practice, or an acting out of the drug raids by police on their estate? What difference do these considerations make to the assessments that educators might make?

Making
Assessment
Work

ACTIVITY 1E   **Toys from the shops**

INTRODUCTION TO THE ACTIVITY

In your workplace you will probably provide a variety of play materials, home-made and bought, natural and manufactured, traditional and up-to-the-minute, purpose-built and improvised. The opportunity for children to form worthwhile concepts and attitudes from developmentally appropriate toys is an important consideration for the educators who select the toys. But some toys may have undesirable effects; they may limit children's understanding, or their access to knowledge; some toys may shape or reinforce stereotyped behaviours, perhaps even affecting children's life choices. The selection of toys available is a vital part of the curriculum in action; it has a direct effect on children's learning and development and on the assessments that educators make of them.

In this activity you will:

- think about why you value certain kinds of play and not others

- think about why you value certain toys and not others

- think about some of the limitations that certain toys might create for children's learning and development

- discuss and evaluate what children might learn from some commercially available toys

Oh dear, William's playing with the death ray gun again. I wish he'd let Samantha have a turn

ACTIVITY 1E   Toys from shops

1. Working alone, look at the Handout **Toys from shops**, showing ten different kinds of toys (or the real life examples, if you and your colleagues have collected them for this activity).
    Use the Handout **Grading Toys** to record your first reactions to these toys, using the grades given on the Handout and adding extra comments to express your feelings.

2. Compare your responses with one other person, explaining why you feel as you do. Which of these descriptions most closely matches each kind of toy - according to you? and to your partner?

3. Work together as a whole group to draw some general conclusions from your discussion so far.

    •   What toys and materials would you include and exclude in your ideal setting for young children? Why?

    •   What sorts of play would you encourage - or discourage - in your ideal setting for young children? Why?

    •   What criteria would you use for selecting toys for your ideal setting for young children? Why?

    •   Record the whole group's thoughts on a flipchart sheet.

Making
Assessment
Work

4.   Choosing toys for an ideal setting is different from what happens in the real world. Work together to think about some of the difficulties that may arise, in your own home and in your workplace.

These suggestions may help to get you going:

'Sometimes grandparents give inappropriate presents. If a grandparent gave my child a ....

'Sometimes people donate inappropriate toys .... If a parent brought in a ....

'Children often bring things from home. When a child brings a ....

'But children **must** play. So long as the children like it ....

'You can't refuse a gift or a contribution. People would feel hurt ....

'It's all the same to the children. They make up their own minds what to do with the toys ....

Add your conclusions to the list on the flip chart sheet.

5.   Work in small groups, drawing on these general conclusions, to think about the connections between your views of worthwhile toys/play and your assessments of children's play.

For example, if you observe children playing with Cindy and Barbie dolls, how do your values and attitudes affect your assessments? How do you respond to these two possibilities?

A

S's play today shows she is learning to be feminine, in the way her family expects her to be. This is a worthwhile part of her development, and I will try and encourage it.

B

S's play today shows she is quickly learning a narrow view of what it is to be female in our society. This may limit her life choices and I will discourage this kind of play in the future.

In what ways do your observations and assessments of children's play reflect your values, attitudes and beliefs?

I can't stand computers. They frighten me to death. I'm NOT having one in my nursery.

But our children will be growing up in the 21st Century

They must have the chance to start learning now ....

Making Assessment Work

Toys to encourage:

fantasy play?
rough and tumble play?
aggression and hatred?
an exploration of powerful feelings?

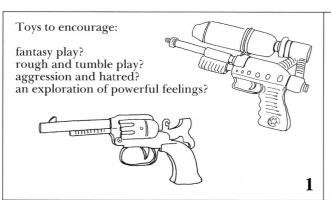

1

Plastic toys for babies in bright primary colours

Teaching a range of skills?
Keeping babies happy for hours?
Offering limited experiences of texture,
smell, temperature,
taste and weight?

2

A tokenistic Black doll that may reinforce racist attitudes and stereotypes?

A realistic Black doll that may promote positive images of Black people?

3

Animate or inanimate?

Toys which represent useful objects transformed into animate creatures?
Appealing toys?
Tricking toddlers into thinking that objects have feelings?
Age appropriate?
Or playing them false?

4

Toys that create magical memories?
Part of your children's cultural heritage?
Out-moded?
Remote?
Irrelevant?

5

A construction kit with feminine appeal

A toy to challenge stereotypes to reinforce them?

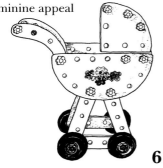

6

the current fashion fad or collectable

Toys that stimulate children's fantasies?
Toys that exploit children's crazes?
Toys that have purely commercial purposes?

7

Barbie, Cindy and their friends

Sex role stereotyping?
Learning gender roles?

8

Sit-and-ride fire engine with all the trimmings

A toy to feed a child's fantasy?
A toy to limit a child's dreams?

9

A pocket money toy from the newsagent

A cheap toy?
An exciting toy for a few days for a child interested in rotation?

10

LOOKING AT VALUES

Toy	Grade	Comments	
		In my workplace	In my family
1			
2			
3			
4			
5			
6			
7			
8			
9			
10			

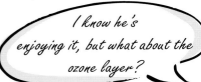

I know he's enjoying it, but what about the ozone layer?

Making Assessment Work

GRADE

1   Yes, I've got one just like it at my place, and it's wonderful

2   Nice, if you have the money to spare

3   OK, it can't do any harm

4   No thanks, I would rather not ......

5   Never. Over my dead body. Absolutely No.

ACTIVITY 1F   Hiroki - A child-like child?

PREPARATION

Re-read the introduction to this section p1.1
Copies of the three Handouts

BEFORE THE MEETING

If possible group members should read the first Handout **Hiroki at pre-school** and the introduction to the activity before the meeting

1 hour 30 minutes

Notes to Group Leaders

This is a long and challenging activity, and it is important to make sure that there is enough time to work through all the stages of the discussion. There is a lot to read in the activity, and some of it would be best done in advance; if this is not possible, you will need to allocate extra time.

INTRODUCTION TO THE ACTIVITY

'To be a (mature) person, we must taste each other's rice.' (Japanese proverb) In this activity you will be able to think about what you are looking for when you assess learning and development. You will ask yourself if what you look for is universal for all young children, or whether it is based on your personal expectations, expectations that reflect your experiences in childhood, your culture and your nationality.

To do this, you will use an observation from a cross-cultural study of three pre-school programmes in Japan, China and the USA. Video-tapes were made of a typical day in each pre-school and were discussed and analysed by cross-national groups of educators, trainers, managers and psychologists.

You will read an account of one child, Hiroki, during one day in a Japanese pre-school. By 'tasting each other's rice', by sharing perceptions with early years educators from other nations, it is possible to learn more about our own approaches, our own values and beliefs, as well as understanding more about pre-school practices in other cultures

The purposes of this activity are for you to:

- examine one short example of practice in a Japanese pre-school

- reflect on similarities and differences in your own approach

- identify some of the characteristics of young children that are central to your view of early years care and education

- become clearer about the values and beliefs that underly your practices

Making Assessment Work

1. Spend some time alone (preferably before the meeting) reading the observation of Hiroki (**Handout 1F Hiroki at Pre-School**)
Work in groups of three or four to discuss your first impressions, and your reactions to Hiroki and his educators' ways of working with him.

2. Read the second Handout **Comments on Hiroki.** Continue the discussion by comparing your ideas and feelings about Hiroki and his behaviour with those of the early years educators in China, Japan and the USA quoted on the Handout. Look for agreements and disagreements, and refer back to the observation of Hiroki for supporting evidence for your views.

3. Come together as a whole group to reflect on the discussion so far. The following questions may be useful:

   • Was it possible to establish a consensus of opinion in your small group? If not, why not?

   • If you were to have an exchange year working in Japan, in Hiroki's pre-school, how would you feel about becoming a member of the staff team?

   • If Fukui-sensei (Hiroki's teacher) came on an exchange to your workplace for a year, how would you benefit from her experience and knowledge? What would she find strange or unexpected in your workplace?

4. During the discussion between the Japanese, Chinese and American educators (which became very heated at times), the Japanese teachers were asked what kind of child they were trying to produce. They replied, unhesitatingly, 'Kodomorashii Kodomo' - a child-like child!

   What is your definition of a child-like child?
   Use the third Handout **What is a child-like child?,** and work on your own for five-ten minutes to complete the sentences.

   Compare your responses with one other person, listening carefully to each other's opinions. You are both describing some of your expectations and assumptions about the kind of person that you believe a young child should be. You are describing the characteristics of what you take to be a normal child, a 'child-like child'.

5. Come together as a whole group to compare your perceptions of 'a child-like child'. Consider how these perceptions, sometimes unspoken, but still deeply held, might affect your interactions, your observations and your assessments.

HANDOUT 1F Hiroki at pre-school

Taken from *Pre-school in Three Cultures* by Tobin, J. J. Wu, D. and Davidson, D. (1989) Yale University Press pp 18-21.

DEALING WITH A DIFFICULT CHILD

On the day we videotaped at Komatsudani, Hiroki started things off with a flourish by pulling his penis out from under the leg of his shorts and waving it at the class during the morning welcome song. During the workbook session that followed, Hiroki called out answers to every question the teacher asked and to many she did not ask. When not volunteering answers, Hiroki gave a loud running commentary on his workbook progress ('now I'm coloring the badger, now the pig ....') as he worked rapidly and deftly on his assignment. He alternated his play-by-play announcing with occasional songs, entertaining the class with loud, accurate renditions of their favourite cartoon themes, complete with accompanying dancing, gestures, and occasional instrumental flourishes. Despite the demands of his singing and announcing schedule, Hiroki managed to complete his workbook pages before most of the older children (of course, those sitting near him might have finished their work faster had they a less distracting tablemate).

Work completed, Hiroki threw his energies wholeheartedly into his comedy routine, holding various colored crayons up to the front of his shorts and announcing that he had a blue, then a green, and finally a black penis. We should perhaps mention at this point that penis and butt jokes were immensely popular with four-year-old children in nearly every school we visited in all three countries. The only noticeable difference was that such humour was most openly exhibited in Japan, where the teachers generally said nothing and sometimes even smiled, whereas American teachers tended to say something like 'We'd rather not hear that kind of talk during group time,' and in China such joking appeared to have been driven largely underground, out of adult view.

As the children lined up to have Fukui-sensei check their completed work, Hiroki fired a barrage of pokes, pushes, and little punches at the back of the boy in front of him, who took it all rather well. In general, as Hiroki punched and wrestled his way through the day with various of his male classmates, they reacted by seeming to enjoy his attentions, by becoming irritated but not actually angry, or, most commonly, by shrugging them off with a 'That's Hiroki for you' sort of expression. The reaction of Satoshi, who cried when Hiroki hit him and stepped on his hand, was the exception to this rule.

During the singing of the prelunch song, Hiroki, who was one of the four daily lunch monitors, abandoned his post in front of the organ to wrestle with a boy seated nearby. While eating, Hiroki regaled his classmates with more songs and

Making Assessment Work

jokes. Finishing his lunch as quickly as he had his workbook, Hiroki joined other fast diners on the balcony, where he roughhoused with some other boys and then disrupted a game by throwing flash cards over the railing to the ground below. The other children seemed more amused than annoyed by these antics, although one girl, Midori, ran inside to tattle to the teacher, who was by now sweeping up under tables. Fukui-sensei sent Midori back to the balcony with some instructions. A few minutes later Fukui-sensei walked out to the balcony, looked over the railing, and said, 'So that's where the cards are going'. Soon several of the children, with the conspicuous exception of Hiroki, ran down the steps to retrieve the fallen cards. This proved to be a losing battle as Hiroki continued to rain cards down upon them. It was now that Hiroki (purposely) stepped on Satoshi's hand, which made him cry. Satoshi was quickly ushered away from the scene by Midori, the girl who had earlier reported the card throwing. Midori, arm around Satoshi's neck, listened very empathetically to his tale of woe and then repeated it several times with gestures to other girls who came by: 'Hiroki threw cards over the balcony and then he stepped on Satoshi's hand, and then he punched Satoshi like this.' The girls then patted Satoshi on the back, suggesting that in the future he find someone other than Hiroki to play with.

Lunch over and the room cleaned up, Fukui-sensei returned to the balcony where, faced with the sight of Hiroki and another boy involved in a fight (which consisted mostly of other boy's being pushed down and climbed on by Hiroki), she said neutrally, 'Are you still fighting?' Then she added, a minute later, in the same neutral tone, 'Why are you fighting anyway?' and told everyone still on the balcony, 'Hurry up and clean up (the flash cards). Lunchtime is over. Hurry, hurry.' Hiroki was by now disrupting the card clean-up by rolling on the cards and putting them in his mouth, but when he tried to enter the classroom Fukui-sensei put her hand firmly on his back and ushered him outside again. Fukui-sensei, who by now was doing the greatest share of of the card picking-up, several times blocked Hiroki from leaving the scene of his crime, and she playfully spanked him on the behind when he continued to roll on the cards.

The rest of the day wound down for Hiroki in similar fashion. At one point in the afternoon Komatsudani's assistant principal, Higashino-sensei, came over to Hiroki and talked softly but seriously to him for three or four minutes, presumably about his behaviour. During the free playground period that ends the day, Hiroki played gently with a toddler and more roughly with some of the older boys. He was finally picked up shortly before 6:00 by his father, making him one of the last children to go home.

Making Assessment Work

Taken from *Pre-School in Three Cultures* by Tobin, J. J. Wu, D. and Davidson, D. (1989) Yale University Press p12-17

SOME COMMENTS ARISING FROM THE OBSERVATION OF HIROKI:

- Staff team at Hiroki's school:

'We think Fukui-sensei (Hiroki's teacher) dealt with Hiroki in a satisfactory way. We think it is right to ignore the most provocative, aggressive and exhibitionist actions. This is a strategy we have agreed on.'

- Higashino - assistant principal of Hiroki's school:

'We should not punish Hiroki. He has pride and he will be hurt if we yell at him or make him sit alone. We must avoid confronting or censuring Hiroki'.

- American cameraman - researcher:

'It was difficult to keep up a posture of scholarly neutrality and not tell Hiroki to "cut it out!" '

- Dana Davidson, author, teacher trainer and child development authority working in assessment and in programmes for gifted children, USA:

'Hiroki is bored, he finishes his work quickly, his behaviour is an attempt to make things more exciting, better matched to the pace and level of stimulation he needs. He is gifted, talented, intelligent.'

- Fukui-sensei - Hiroki's Japanese teacher:

'Hiroki is not especially intelligent; if he is so clever, why doesn't he understand better? If he understood better, he would behave better'.

- Chinese teacher:

'Why are the teachers so easy on a boy who is so spoiled, a boy so used to having his own way and monopolising so much of his class's energy and attention?'

- Higashino:

'Hiroki has an emotional problem. He has no mother and so he has not learned to be dependent. That is why he does not know how to be obedient and sensitive to others'.

- Researchers to Hiroki's teachers:

'Is it not a problem for the other children that Hiroki causes so much chaos in the classroom? He uses up a disproportionate amount of staff time and energy'.

- Yoshizawa, principal of Hiroki's school:

'No, I would say just the opposite. The children in that class are lucky to have Hiroki there. He makes things interesting!'

- Higashino:

'By learning how to deal with a child like Hiroki they learn to be more complete human beings. If the children find Hiroki a problem, they will learn to deal with him and Hiroki will learn more from the disapproval of his classmates than from a reprimand from his teacher'.

- Yoshizawa:

'Misbehaving, including fighting, is a lost art for today's sheltered nuclear-family raised children.'

- Fukui-sensei:

'I let the boys fight because it is natural for boys of that age to fight, and it is good for them to have the experience while they are young of what it feels like to fight ....'

(There is lots more debate in the book!)

HANDOUT 1F   **What is a child-like child?**

Working on your own, please complete these sentences.

When a child is fighting, I ....

When a child throws play materials, I ....

When a child makes a mess (with paint/water, mud), I ....

When a child is angry, I ....

When a child is sad, I ....

When a child is frightened, I ....

I would never stop a child ....

I would never ask a child ....

I would never read a child ....

I would never allow a child to (do) ....

I would never allow a child to have ....

When a child ....I call that naughty

When a child ....I call that rude

If I saw/heard a child ....I would be really worried

ACTIVITY 1G   A long way from home

PREPARATION

Pens and paper
Copies of the policy statement given below, if required

about 45 minutes

Notes to Group Leaders

In the course of this activity you may find it useful to refer to the following extract from a statement describing the values that underpin the work of the Early Childhood Unit at the National Children's Bureau.

THE UNIT BELIEVES THAT:

...... children develop to their full potential only if they live in an environment which reflects their individual identity, culture and heritage, and in which positive action is taken to support this .....

.... we live in a pluralist society, in which children will grow up in many different types and forms of family, reflecting their values and beliefs. We need to recognise and be sensitive to these, whilst acknowledging that the needs of children must be our prime concern.

INTRODUCTION TO THE ACTIVITY

In this activity you will have the opportunity to go a little further with your discussion of alternative approaches to early childhood care and education.

You will be able to:

- continue your exploration of the values and beliefs that underly your practice

- consider how your value system fits into, and takes account of, the pluralist society in which we live

Making Assessment Work

ACTIVITY 1G   A long way from home

1. Imagine that a group of educators from Japan, China or the USA have come on an exchange visit to your workplace. They are a long way from home, and will find many strange and unfamiliar things to think about. Work in a small group to consider these questions:

    • what might they comment on to each other privately?
    • what might they ask you about?
    • which parts of your practice might seem very strange to them?

2. Continue the discussion by looking at some more general questions. Working in four small groups, select one question from the following, so that each group is considering a different aspect of the topic.

A	Is the provision in your workplace typical for all young children in Britain? In England? In Wales? In any city? In any rural area? In your particular local authority?
B	Which aspects of your practice do you think are specifically matched to the community and families with whom you work?
C	Which aspects of your practice seem to you to have national characteristics? Are they important?
D	When you visit other early years settings in this country, do you generally think: 'This is very similar to my workplace' or 'Goodness, this is a different approach.'

3. Come together as a whole group to listen to a brief report on each question that has been discussed.

    To wind up the discussion, consider this final question:

    Would the quality of education and care for young children be improved if every daycare setting was different? Or if they were all practically identical?

Making Assessment Work

But. Oh, gosh

Well that may be how you do it in West Hartlepool, but here in East Hartlepool, we ...... would never ....not even possibly

ACTIVITY 1H	**Dustbin day**

1 hour 30 minutes

PREPARATION

Copies of the Handout
Pens and paper
Copies of the outcomes of the other activities used throughout
this section

Notes to Group Leaders

This activity will encourage group members to review their own learning and to talk about the implications for change in their practice as a result of their work on this section. You will be able to encourage members to identify the ideas, attitudes and values that they have modified, revised or rejected, ready to put in the dustbin.

It is important to remind group members that change, flexibility, and a continuous quest for new ways of working are strengths, not weaknesses. But it is not always easy to admit you have changed your mind, and so the group leader's role may be to listen and reflect the guilty, sad, or confused feelings expressed by group members, as they face the need for changes in their work with children.

INTRODUCTION TO THE ACTIVITY

In this activity you will be able to think about the ways in which your values and beliefs have changed during the time you've been working with children - and, perhaps, during the time you've been bringing up your own children.

You will be able to:

* identify values and practices you
  have modified and discarded

* identify the basic principles that you
  would never abandon

*Making
Assessment
Work*

1. Think back to your first experiences of working with children, and try to identify some parts of your practice that you think have changed. Use the incomplete sentences on the Handout to get you started.

2. Now work in small groups to talk about these changes in your practice. Think about how your practice changed: whose influence was it? What experiences made you rethink? Did you move to a very different setting or community?

3. Select some of the areas of your work where you have identified some changes in your approach, and think about the ideas that underlie this part of your practice. Look at the reasons for the change, asking yourself and each other:

    '**Why** have I/you changed in this way?'

    Make notes under two headings, THEN and NOW.

    For example:

THEN

I used to believe it was really important for the children to use a knife and fork because ....

I used to ban guns and war play, because ....

I used to insist they were out of nappies in my playgroup because ...

NOW

But now I believe ....

because ....

But now I believe....
because ....

But now I believe .....

because ....

Other areas of practice that were discussed by groups using the trial version of this pack included:

Naming the letters of the alphabet
Fighting
Crying
Cuddling
Displaying children's work
Reading stories to large groups

Making Assessment Work

4. When I'm clearing out cupboards, I sometimes come across things that I know I ought to throw out - but somehow I can't quite bring myself to. Are there ideas in our head that we feel like this about?

and it might come in useful

and it doesn't take up much room

but it was my granny's

So I think I'll keep it!

I know its broken

5. In contrast, each of us holds firm to a few, a very few, basic values that we would never abandon. To end your work on this section, read back over the activities that you have completed so far, trying to summarise for yourself what you learned from each one. You may also want to re-read the introduction to this whole section on **Looking at values**, to remind yourself of where you started and what the purposes of all these activities have been.

   Now try to put into words the two or three ideas that are at the centre of your work with children - the values that are 'Not for Sale', under any circumstances. Write your statements where every one can see them.

6. Discuss your statements with the rest of the group.

   Keep these statements in a safe place. You will work on them again later in the pack.

TO THE STAKE

I didn't think anyone cared so much about my values!

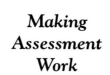

Making Assessment Work

HANDOUT 1H   **Dustbin day**

Working on your own, look back to your first experience of working with young children and complete these sentences.

I remember spending a lot of time on ....
....

I always used to ....
....

I insisted on ....
....

I was determined never to ....
....

I made a point of...
....

It was a struggle but I managed to ....
....

I was rather fussy about ....
....

I used to get flustered when ....
....

I didn't know what to do when..
....

I was completely thrown by ....
....
....
....
....

SECTION ONE: LOOKING AT VALUES

The main themes of this section have been:

all forms of assessment are based on an implicit value system, a set of beliefs about children

in assessing young children's learning and development, educators draw on their beliefs about what children should do, say, feel and be

assessment practices will be more effective if educators explore their values, understand them more fully, and make them explicit

REFERENCES

Forster, M. (1988) *Elizabeth Barrett Browning A Biography* Chatto & Windus

Tobin, J.J., Wu D., & Davidson, D. (1989) *Pre-School in Three Cultures* Yale University Press

Dixon, B. (1990) *Playing Them False. A Study of Children's toys, games & puzzles* Trentham Books

Goldstein, J. (1992) *"War Toys" A Review of Empirical Research* Published in association with The British Toy and Hobby Association

Gosse, E. (1907) *Father and Son* Heinmann Reissued Penguin Modern Classics 1970

Lifton, B. J. (1989) *The King of Children* Pan Books

Paley, V. G. (1984) *Boys and Girls: Superheroes in the Doll Corner* University of Chicago Press

Wharton, E. (1928) *The Children* Appleton & Co. Reissland (1985) Virago

Winnicott, D. W. (1964) *The Child, the Family and the Outside World* Penguin Books (Reprinted 1991)

SECTION 2

About feelings

2

Making
Assessment
Work

INTRODUCTION

Helping children to have a sense of their own self-worth, encouraging them to believe that they are special, capable, unique individuals, helping them to recognise and accept the importance of their feelings about themselves and other people: these are some of the most difficult and challenging tasks all early years educators undertake. And if we are to do these things effectively, we need to think carefully about children's emotional development, and about how their feelings are affected by our words and deeds - and feelings.

This pack is about the process of assessment - what we do and what we might do. But assessing and being assessed is never a cold, dispassionate experience. Both assessor and assessed are emotionally involved in what is going on, and these emotions are rooted in very deep feelings about ourselves as individuals. As we assess the children in our care, they bring to the experience all that they have learned about themselves, their sense of self-esteem or lack of it. And we, the adults, do the same.

The purposes of this section are for you to

*   explore some challenging questions about the feelings involved in assessment

*   think about the feelings of a person - child or adult - who is being assessed

*   think about the feelings of the person who is doing the assessing

*   understand more about the emotional dimension of assessment for everyone involved - parents, children and educators

There are eight activities in this section, from which you will need to select at least three or four. Three of them (B, C, D) are mostly about children's feelings; four of them are mostly about adults' feelings (E, F, G and H). The first activity forms a short introduction to the section.

about 20 minutes

ACTIVITY 2A	**A day in the life of...**

PREPARATION

Pens and notebooks

Notes to Group Leaders

You may wish to remind group members of whatever agreement you have made on confidentiality. Some group members may feel anxious about talking about their emotions if they think their privacy is being threatened. You may want to reassure them that this is a brief, small-group discussion, not group therapy or the Grand Inquisition!

INTRODUCTION TO THE ACTIVITY

In this short activity you will be able to talk confidentially with one or two people about some of the feelings that adults and children experience, inside and outside your workplace.

The purpose of the activity is to help you to

* recognise the wealth of emotional experience that is part of everyday life

* acknowledge the range of emotions experienced by others - educators, parents and children

* think about the feelings (adults' and children's) that are hard to express and that sometimes stay hidden

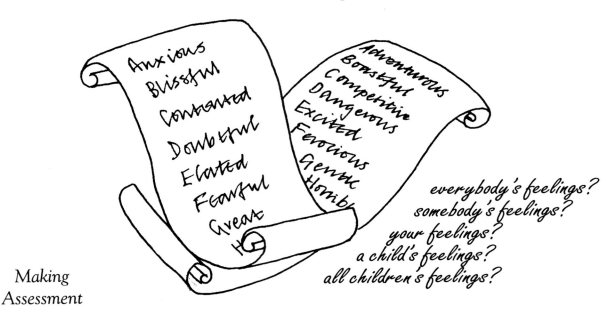

*Making
Assessment
Work*

ACTIVITY 2A   A day in the life of...

1.   Working on your own, think back over your last weekend, and make some quick notes of all the different feelings that you experienced.

2.   Work in a small group to compare notes and to produce a long list of the feelings that adults ordinarily experience, at home and in the workplace. Think about other adults you know, both family and friends: do they have feelings you haven't listed yet?

3.   Think about some of the children you know well, in your workplace or in your family. Does the list you have just written match the feelings that they experience? Are there other words to add to the list? Or to cross off? Do they have as wide a range of feelings as you? Wider? Narrower?

     If you work with babies or very young children, consider whether a list of their feelings would be any different from a list for older children.

4.   Now think about the ways in which you express your feelings. Do you tell your colleagues what you feel? Or do you tend to keep your feelings to yourself? Think about why you express some feelings but not others.

5.   What about your colleagues, family and friends? Do you always know what they are feeling?

     And what about the children? Do they tell you how they feel? Or do you infer it from their faces, their bodies, their movements? Or do they keep some of their feelings hidden?

     Are some feelings much more private than others? For adults? For children?

     Think about the possible reasons for this.

Making
Assessment
Work

about 45 minutes

PREPARATION

Pens and notebooks

Notes to Group Leaders

Some group members may find it difficult or impossible to remember 'labels' from their own childhood. As a way of getting started on this activity, you might consider giving each member a prepared label or badge to wear, using some of the suggestions on the next page. Be sure to give yourself a badge! A group leader who did this during the trialling of the pack wrote: 'I wore a label that said 'Idiot!' I was surprised at the feelings this aroused in me - it helped the whole group to share their childhood experiences quite easily.'

INTRODUCTION TO THE ACTIVITY

What did adults call you, when you were little? Not all labels are deliberately cruel, but they all tell children something about who they are expected to be, and how they are expected to behave. In this activity, you will be able to

- think about your own feelings about being 'labelled' by adults

- think about how the young children you work with now may feel about the names that they are called by their friends, family and educators

Mary Jane, you're a cry-baby!

that's what you are

cry baby!

bye Baby Bunting

yah!

Making Assessment Work

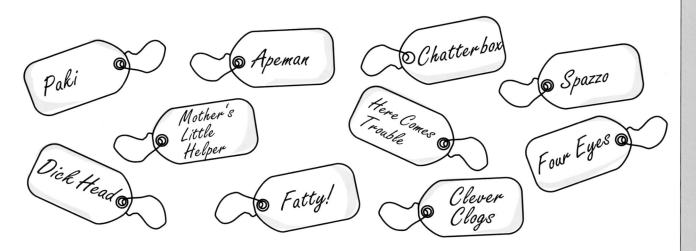

1. Working on your own, make a list of the labels you remember from your own childhood. Talk about what you have written with one other person.

2. Work in small groups to think about:

    •   how these labels made you feel, when you were little

    •   how these labels make you feel now

    •   how you feel when you hear another child being labelled like this

    •   whether you can recognise in yourself the feelings of the child you once were

    •   whether you sometimes recognise yourself and your feelings in the young children you work with

3. In the whole group discuss the ways in which the children you work with may experience being 'labelled', at home or in your workplace. How do they feel? How do they express their feelings? How do you respond?

45 minutes

ACTIVITY 2C	Don't be silly

PREPARATION

Pens and notebooks

INTRODUCTION TO THE ACTIVITY

In this activity you will be able to think about some occasions in your childhood when your feelings were denied by adults. The purpose of the activity is for you to

- consider the possible effects of denying children's feelings

- think about the most appropriate ways of responding to children's feelings

ACTIVITY 2C   Don't be silly

1.   Working in pairs, talk together about the times when you told - or tried to show - an adult how you were feeling and heard in reply something like this!

It's a nice doggy

Don't be silly!

Cheer up!

Oh, no, it's not as bad as all that!

Look Susan's not crying ...

You can't be hungry again!

But they're lovely new glasses ...

What a nasty temper

Talk about how these incidents made you feel.

2.   Spend a little time thinking about what you would have liked to have heard instead.

3.   Now join with another pair to think more generally about what happens to children when their feelings are denied. Draw on your experiences but try to list some general points about the possible effects of denial on the growth of children's understanding of themselves.

4.   Bring the discussion to a close by thinking about alternatives: what could be done instead? Are there ways in which adults can:

recognise?
      accept?
           acknowledge?
                  understand?
                         reflect children's feelings?

Are these alternatives more appropriate? In what way?

5.   Make a few notes in each group of four about these different possibilities, which you will be able to use in the next activity.

Making Assessment Work

about 1 hour 15 minutes

ACTIVITY 2D	In response

PREPARATION

Pens and notebooks
Copies of the Handout, or a selection of items from this Handout together with further examples provided by you and/or the group members, with age-appropriate examples

INTRODUCTION TO THE ACTIVITY

In this activity you will be able to think about different ways of responding to children's expressions of feeling. You will be able to think about your own emotional response to what your children show or tell you about their feelings.

The purpose of the activity is for you to

* review a range of possible responses to children's feelings

* think about why some responses are more appropriate than others

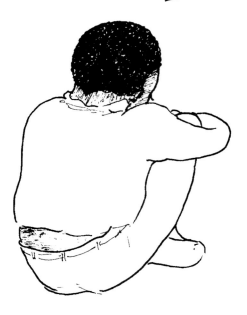

Nobody understands me
Nobody listens to me
Nobody wants to make the world a better place for me to live in
Nobody ....

ACTIVITY 2D　　　　　　In response

1. Working as a group, organise yourselves into pairs, each of whom will work on one or two of the examples given on the Handout. Try to ensure that every example is covered. Taking one example at a time, list as many possible responses as you can to the child and her or his emotions. This is an opportunity to think about a range of responses, including what **other** people might do, not just what you would typically do, or your first gut reaction.

2. Now arrange these possibilities in order, from the **most** appropriate (according to you) to the **least** appropriate. Use your jotted notes from the last activity to help you here. Try to be critical, as gently as you can, of your suggested responses, as you search for the most appropriate.

3. Work with one other pair to discuss the responses you have invented and the ranking you have given them. Be sure to ask each other 'Why?', gently, but firmly, as often as you can.

4. Review your discussion so far, by choosing one of the emotions you have been discussing (for example: anger, envy, frustration) and work together to write a sentence with this format:

When a child shows ANGER,

it is best for an adult to ....

but not to ....

because...

(Use this same format for
ENVY
FRUSTRATION
FEAR
IMPATIENCE
and so on.)

I'm really angry because you won't believe I'm angry ....

Once again, during this part of the discussion, it is important for you to feel able to challenge others - and yourself - about appropriate responses. What we might do without really thinking about it may be very different from what we would do if we had more time to consider. In these imaginary situations, we do have a little more time - so we must use it well!

5. If there is time, complete two or three such sentences, before comparing your work with another group of four. Look carefully at each other's work, and think back to the notes you made in the last activity about the possibilities of recognition, acceptance, acknowledgement and understanding. Are these possibilities reflected in your work?

6. This is one of those discussions that can never be concluded once and for all. You may find that you go on thinking about some of the issues raised long after the session ends. And in the next few days you may notice some incidents in your workplace that you would like to bring to a continued discussion. You may want to arrange a short follow up session at the start of your next meeting.

Making Assessment Work

Please use this list as a starting point: select the ones you want to discuss and add more incidents from your own experience of children communicating their feelings.

1. A 14-month-old has a tantrum because another child has taken his personal blanket from his sleeping mattress.

2. A two-year-old shows great fear, crying and screaming at the sight and sound of the toilet flushing.

3. A nine-month-old baby crawls to a brick building made by older children and shows surprise and pleasure as she demolishes the construction.

4. A four-year-old regularly masturbates during group story time.

5. A six-month-old baby cries bitterly while waiting for his bottle to be made up.

6. A two-year-old is fiercely insistent about unpacking the shopping, including eggs and bottles. She refuses to be helped.

7. An 18-month-old is inconsolable after his 'nou-nou' (treasured object) has been mislaid. He rejects all substitutes.

8. A six-year-old takes a violent dislike to a new member of staff, which she expresses noisily: 'I hate Miss B. She smells.'

9. A five-year-old is very distressed at parting from his father at the beginning of the session. The child's prolonged crying upsets some of the others.

10. A three-year-old runs into the nursery excitedly whirling his arms and making loud helicopter rotary blade noises. His exuberant antics knock over the black paint and drown a quiet story in the corner. 'I am the fastest and bestest' he asserts.

11. Four-year-old twins spend all their time together, holding hands and cuddling. They refuse, absolutely, to be separated. They make no approaches to other children, and show great distress if other children approach them.

12. A six-year-old stomps off angrily from a board game shouting, 'You cheat! You always win, it's not fair, I won't be your friend any more.'

ACTIVITY 2E   Am I a worm?

PREPARATION

Pens and notebooks

INTRODUCTION TO THE ACTIVITY

Most of us spend at least some of our time running ourselves down. Some of the things we say about ourselves may be justified, but probably not all of them.

In this activity you will be able to:

* explore some of the reasons why you talk about yourselves in this way

* think about ways in which you might cope with occasional feelings of inadequacy

* discuss how you might help children to have realistic perceptions of themselves

1 hour

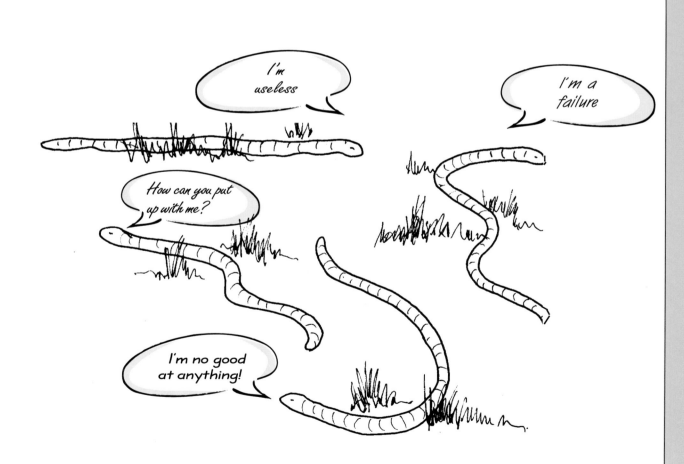

ACTIVITY 2E   Am I a worm?

1.   Working in small groups of two or three, make a list of all the self-critical things that you regularly say about yourself. If you are working with people who know you well, they will probably be able to add to your list, from having heard you carry on over the years!

For example:

> I'm no good at mathematics
> I'm hopeless at drawing
> I haven't got anything to say in the big group
> I'm always behind with my work
> I'm dreadfully disorganised
> I'm so sorry I'm late again

2.   Now work together to discuss these questions:

*   Are these things we think for ourselves, or have we heard other people say them about us?

*   When did we start learning to say these things?

*   How does saying these things make us feel?

*   Does saying these things make us any better - at being punctual, or more organised, for example?

*   What are the hidden messages we are trying to convey when we say these things?

> I'm frightened

> You intimidate me!

> Don't expect too much!

> I've failed so often before

> You're better than me

> miles better at everything

Making Assessment Work

ACTIVITY 2E   Am I a worm?

3. Next, consider whether there are any positive things we
   can say about ourselves? - with **conviction!**

How does saying **these** things make us feel?

4. When you have spent some time thinking about some of
   the ways in which you think about yourself, move the
   discussion back to the young children you work with.

   • What sorts of positive things would you like to hear
     children say about themselves?

   • What sorts of negative things that children say about
     themselves would worry you?

   • What sorts of negative things would be appropriate
     for them to say about themselves?

5. Now it is important to think about the part that adults can
   play in helping children to have realistic perceptions of
   themselves.

   How can you encourage children to believe in their
   powers and capabilities? What can you say? What can you
   do?

*I may look
like a worm, but that's
not how I feel.*

And you may have time to conclude this activity by
thinking about the ways in which we can help each other
- our adult colleagues - to feel the same way.

*Making
Assessment
Work*

about 45 minutes

PREPARATION

Pens and notebooks
Large sheets of paper, with some sheets marked off into four sections
Thick felt-tips
Blutak

INTRODUCTION

In this activity, you will be able to think about the emotional impact - and outcomes - of assessment.

You will ask yourself and each other:

* How does the process of assessment affect the person being assessed?

* Before, during and after? Even long after?

Making Assessment Work

ACTIVITY 2F   Being assessed

1. Working on your own, make a few notes about two occasions in your life (as a child, or an adult) when you were assessed. Choose one occasion when the assessment was very *positive and encouraging*, and one when it was *negative and discouraging*. We were all assessed often enough at school but it's worth trying to remember some of the other settings in which assessment takes place. It isn't only teachers who assess us - but also our family and friends! For example, in a driving lesson, singing in a choir, going for a job, meeting your in-laws for the first time, your granny's view of you when you were little, a birthday tea for your children ....

2. Share your notes with one other person and then work in fours to think about these two questions for each of the incidents you have described.

    •   What did you feel?

    •   What did you learn?

    Record your discussion on a big sheet of paper, showing positive feelings and learning in one column, and the negative feelings and learning in another.

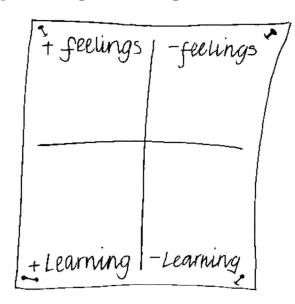

3. Pin your sheets up so that everyone can see them and spend a little time talking about what you have found out.

4. In your original pairs, try to summarise this discussion in two sentences - one about the positive effects of assessment and one about the negative. Write your sentences where the whole group can see them - and discuss them.

Making
Assessment
Work

1 hour

| ACTIVITY 2G | Anything but criticism |

PREPARATION

Pens and notebooks
Copies of the Handout
Large sheets of paper, felt tips, Blutak
Copies of 2.19 as further reading

Notes to Group Leaders

If your group members decide to follow up this discussion by making observations in their workplaces, you will need to allow time for them to discuss their findings at a subsequent meeting. It might be useful to keep the large sheets of paper at hand, so that they can be referred to again during the second discussion.

INTRODUCTION

We sometimes tend to assume that praise makes everyone feel good about themselves and that criticism is always unpleasant or painful. And yet this isn't necessarily so. Sometimes praise can be unwelcome, and some friendly, constructive criticism can have a very positive effect on us.

In this activity you will be able to:

* explore the feelings that praise and criticism have aroused in you

* think about how we praise and criticise young children

* think about the possible effects of what we do

*Making
Assessment
Work*

ACTIVITY 2G   Anything but criticism

1. Working on your own, think of some examples of
    praise and criticism: praise that made you feel bad as
    well as good, and criticism that made you feel good as
    well as bad.

2. Working as a large group, collect together the
    characteristics of the four different kinds of praise and
    criticism. Think about the reasons that made you
    respond as you did at the time (for example - 'she is
    someone I respect enormously.' - 'It was so insincere')
    as well as the actual praise or criticism itself. Use large
    sheets of paper, divided up like this, so that everyone's
    contributions can be recorded.

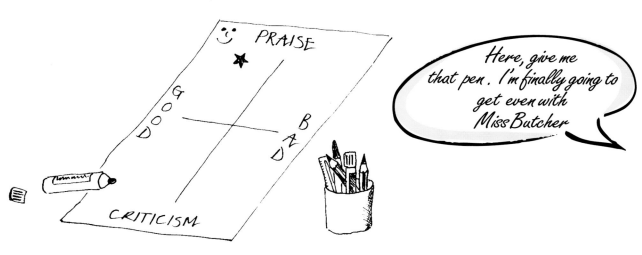

3. When you have talked about each of the four categories
    think about how these different approaches might
    affect the young children in your workplace. Work in
    small groups to shape some guidelines for giving
    worthwhile feedback to young children. For example,
    you might use the format shown on the Handout.

4. Come together as a whole group to share the guidelines
    that you have drafted. Check that you understand
    exactly what other small groups are recommending by
    asking them to give illustrations from their own
    experience. An interesting way of classifying the
    feedback that is given by an adult trainer to the trainee
    is described on p2.19. You may want to look at this now,
    as a way of ending the discussion, or take it away and
    read it later.

5. FOLLOW-UP ACTIVITY: you may decide that you
    need to monitor your own use of praise and criticism in
    your workplace and continue this discussion at a further
    meeting. You might need to watch out for the apparent
    effects of what you say and do, as well as noting your
    own words and actions.

Making
Assessment
Work

ABOUT FEELINGS

Always?! That's a tall order

I just praise everything they do

In our family, we don't praise our children

It does depend on how you're feeling yourself

Some days I do feel grouchy

Mind you, they do have to be TOLD don't they?

But I don't want to criticise children at all!

come off it!

You can never give children too much praise

NEVER's a difficult word it makes me feel anxious

Making Assessment Work

WHEN WE PRAISE WHAT CHILDREN DO, WE MUST TRY

ALWAYS to ....

....

....

....

SOMETIMES to ....

....

....

....

NEVER to ....

....

....

....

WHEN WE CRITICISE WHAT CHILDREN DO, WE MUST TRY

ALWAYS to ....

....

....

....

SOMETIMES to ....

....

....

NEVER to ....

....

....

Try to give some examples of what you might say or do for each of these statements.

Trainers of young adult trainees (in, for example, the clothing industry) are sometimes encouraged to think about the feedback they give using the four-part diagram shown below, which classifies feedback into four types.

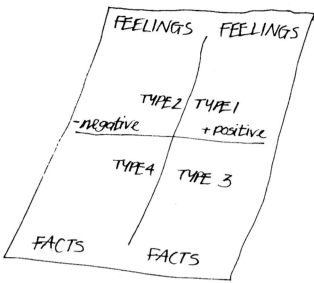

TYPE 1

Feedback that is positive, and expresses approval of the trainee, will make the trainee feel good about him or herself. 'That's lovely'. 'You have done well.' 'Brilliant.' This type of feedback can be effective in establishing a warm and friendly relationship between the trainer and the trainee. But it should not be used to excess.

TYPE 2

Feedback that is negative, and seems to be directed at the trainee personally, will have the opposite effect. The trainees will feed rejected instead of appreciated, and their self-esteem will be diminished. They will feel less secure and more apprehensive about their relationships with the trainer. 'That's terrible'. 'Oh dear, oh dear.' 'What *have* you been doing?' Feedback of this kind is never appropriate.

TYPE 3

This category contains positive feedback that informs trainees about aspects of their work that are successful and effective. It is factual, rather than personal or emotional. 'That seam is perfectly straight.' 'You have fitted the pockets exactly in place.' 'Your finishings are exceptionally neat.' This is the most useful form of feedback, because it enables trainees to learn what it is that they have done well; they learn the criteria for the trainer's assessment of them, and they learn the extent to which they have reached these criteria. This type of feedback gives trainees a feeling of success, but, more importantly, it helps them understand how and why they were successful.

TYPE 4

This is negative feedback that is also factual and informative. 'This edge is crooked because your scissors need sharpening.' 'The tension on the bobbin is too loose and so your stitching is uneven.' 'You have not aligned the edges accurately and the sleeve is set too far forward.' When there is a friendly, trusting relationship between trainer and trainee, this type of feedback is extremely powerful. It is based on the principle that the trainee's feelings will not be hurt by accurate information about the facts of his or her performance. Feedback Type 1 supports positive feelings rather than performance; whereas this negative feedback can act as constructive criticism, stimulating further learning and self-evaluation.

After you have read this description you may want to look again at your earlier work in this activity.

Making
Assessment
Work

at least 1 hour 30 minutes

ACTIVITY 2H	Judge and jury

PREPARATION

Pens and notebooks
Copies of the Handout
Large sheets of paper, felt tips and Blutak
Copies of follow-up material: The Rights of the Child

Susan, I condemn you to three days hard labour and no tricycles

Notes to Group Leaders

This is a long activity, and it is important to allow enough time for group members to follow the stages of the discussion through to the end, without having to hurry over parts that need careful consideration. If time is short, it will be better to do the activity in two parts, at separate meetings.

This is the last activity in this section and so, at the end, it will be worth taking a little time to review the work that has been done so far. There may be a need for some kind of follow-up activity, based on practice in the workplace that needs modifying or developing in the light of new insights. Such developments will need to be discussed at subsequent meetings. A possible follow-up activity is described on p2.23 and this too would need incorporating into your plans for your next meetings.

If you do not choose to follow up this final activity in any way, it will still be worthwhile to conclude work on this section by asking group members to reflect on what they have **learned** and, of course, on how they have **felt** during their work on this section.

Making Assessment Work

ACTIVITY 2H Contd.   Judge and jury

INTRODUCTION TO THE ACTIVITY

The judge on the bench is a very much more powerful person than the prisoner in the dock. Even if the judge acquits the prisoner, after a unanimous verdict of Not Guilty, there is still an enormous gap between them in terms of power and control. Their relationship will never be an equal one.

When we assess young children's learning, we do not dress up in a wig and gown and stand the children in the dock. Nevertheless, the act of assessing is, in a sense, an expression of the power that we have over the children we work with, and their future lives.

In later sections we will look at some of the consequences and outcomes of assessment:
* for the curriculum we provide
* for the children themselves
* for the colleagues who receive our assessments
* for the parents of the children we work with

Here we will briefly consider the impact of assessment on ourselves - as human beings in our own right, and as members of many different relationships in the workplace.

In this activity you will think about:

* your power as an educator

* your responsibilities as an educator

* your rights as an educator

* and how you can act most effectively for the benefit of the children in your care

Making Assessment Work

1. Working on your own, complete the sentences on the Handout provided, and then, working with one other person, compare your first thoughts. Note particularly any examples of mixed feelings in your responses. For example, one early years educator wrote (for number 3) ... 'I feel both proud and humble - this mixture worries me - can't I even make up my mind about myself?'

2. This activity is concerned with the relationship between three key concepts:

RIGHTS — RESPONSIBILITIES — POWER

and with the emotions generated by these three concepts in their everyday application to young children in group settings.

Work in three groups, using what you have written on the handout, to map out all the different emotions that are associated, for assessor and assessed, with one of these concepts (so that one group works on the concept **power,** one on **rights**, one on **responsibilities**).

It may be helpful to do this in the form of speech bubbles or thought balloons, picturing yourselves as:

* an educator who is thinking about the difficulties of exercising his or her **right** to assess children's learning

or

* an educator who is concerned with his or her **responsibility** to assess, with its range, its limitations, its origins

or

* an educator who is reflecting on his or her sense of **power** (or powerlessness), who is also aware of children's powerlessness and power

For example .....

and where does that right come from?

BUT it makes me feel anxious

I DO have the RIGHT to assess.....

When I have to work on my own ....

Isolated - unsupported - uncertain - - determined!

I feel...

Making Assessment Work

ACTIVITY 2H   Judge and jury

3. Working as a whole group, look at the three sheets, and clarify any points that need further explanation. Reflect on the process of discussion so far. How easy do we find it to talk about our own power as educators? What might be the source of any difficulty?

4. David Smail writes of the need for adults in close contact with children to understand the possibility of 'the loving use of power'. Imagine that in your workplace, you and your colleagues have achieved, in your assessment practice, **the loving use of power.**

    •   What would you actually be doing?
    •   What would the children experience?

    Write two lists, as shown below, of the actual events that would illustrate the concept of the 'loving use of power' in action in your workplace.

We the educators would...	*The children would...*
- give lots of real life examples	- give lots of real life examples

5. Bring your work on this section to a close by showing each other your lists. Are these aspirations realistic? You may want to form a Good Resolution for yourself, and commit yourself to carrying it out, based on this discussion.

6. FOLLOW-UP ACTIVITY: one way of extending this discussion, and taking the idea of **rights** a little further, would be to compile a 'Bill of Rights' - or rather two - one from the assessor's point of view, and one from the assessed. You might use a format such as:

The assessor has the right to...	*The child being assessed has the right to ...*

7. You might find the extracts provided as follow-up material useful in your discussion of children's rights.

ABOUT FEELINGS

1. When I am assessing a child's learning, I feel ....
....
....

2. When I write something down about a child, I feel ....
....
....

3. When I think my judgements can help a child, I feel ....
....
....

4. If I thought my judgements could harm a child, I would feel..
....
....

5. The word 'power' makes me think of ....
....
....

6. As an early years educator, I have a responsibility to ....
....
....

7. This responsibility makes me feel ....
....
....

8. As an early years educator, I have the right to ....
....
....

9. This right makes me feel ....
....
....

10. I do not have the right to ....
....
....

11. Children are powerful when ....
....
....

12. Children have the right to ....
....
....

13. If I knew what a difference my assessment might make in 20 years time, I ....
....
....

14. The best way to describe my relationship with the young children I work with is...................
....
....

The Convention On The Rights Of The Child

Adopted by the General Assembly of the United Nations on 20 November 1989 and ratified by the UK in December 1991

Newell, P. (1991) *The United Nations Convention and children's rights in the UK*. National Children's Bureau

Articles

2. Every child has these rights irrespective of race, colour, sex, language, religion, political opinion, disability or any other status, and must be protected against all forms of discrimination or punishment arising from the status of parents or legal guardians.

5. The rights of parents and others responsible for the child to provide appropriate guidance consistent with the child's evolving capacities must be respected.

12. The child has the right to express his or her own views, the views of the child being given due weight in accordance with the age and maturity of the child.

13. The child shall have the right to freedom of expression; this right shall include freedom to seek, receive and impart information and ideas of all kinds, regardless of frontiers, either orally, in writing or in print, in the form of art, or through any other media of the child's choice.

16. The child shall not be subjected to arbitrary or unlawful interference with his or her privacy.

17. The child must have access to information from the mass media and other sources, so we must encourage the production and dissemination of children's books... and have regard to the linguistic needs of the child who also belongs to a minority group.

18. Parents or guardians have primary responsibility for bringing up their children. The State must give them appropriate assistance and ensure the development of facilities and services for the care of children. The children of working parents have the right to benefit from child care services.

23. The mentally or physically disabled child has the right to a full and decent life in conditions which ensure dignity, promote self-reliance, and facilitate the child's active participation in the community, and should have access to education, training, care, rehabilitation, preparation for employment and recreation, where possible free of charge.

29. The aims of education of the child shall be directed to:

-   the development of the child's personality, talents, and mental and physical abilities to their fullest potential.

-   the development of respect for the child's parents, his or her own cultural identity, language and values, for the national values of the country in which the child is living, the country from which he or she may originate, and for civilizations different from his or her own.

-   the preparation of a child for responsible life in a free society, in the spirit of understanding, peace, tolerance, equality and friendship among all people.

-   the development of respect for the natural environment.

30. Children of minorities or indigenous populations shall not be denied the right to enjoy his or her culture, to profess and practise his or her own religion, and to use his or her own language.

31. Children have the right to rest and leisure, to engage in play and recreational activities appropriate to the age of the child, and to participate in a cultural and artistic life.

34. Children must be protected from all forms of sexual exploitation and abuse.

Making
Assessment
Work

Review

SECTION TWO:
ABOUT FEELINGS

The main themes of this section have been:

- children experience a range of feelings, which they express in a variety of ways. Adult educators have the responsibility of finding appropriate ways of acknowledging and responding to these feelings.

- working with young children involves our own feelings as well as our professional expertise.

- the things we do and say when we assess young children's learning affect their feelings, their sense of self-worth, and their knowledge of themselves.

- we bring our own feelings, as adults, to the process of assessment. These feelings may be associated with our experiences of being assessed when we ourselves were children.

- by trying to understand the emotional dimension of assessment, we can learn to work more effectively for the benefit of young children.

REFERENCES

Newell, P. (1991) *The United Nations Convention and Children's Rights in the UK*. National Children's Bureau

Bettelheim, B. (1987) *A Good Enough Parent* Thames and Hudson

Miller, A. (1987) *The Drama of Being a Child* Virago

Miller, A. (1987) *For Your Own Good* Virago

Miller, A. (1990) *Banished Knowledge* Virago

Rogers, C. (1961) *On Becoming a Person* Houghton Miflin

Salzberger-Wittenberg, I., Henry, G. and Osborne, E. (1983) *The Emotional Experience of Teaching and Learning* Routledge and Kegan Paul

Smail, D. (1987) *Taking Care* Dent

SECTION 3
Looking at learning

SECTION THREE LOOKING AT LEARNING

INTRODUCTION

In this section you will be able to explore aspects of your understanding of young children's learning.

As you work on this section with your colleagues, you will be moving towards a shared understanding of how children learn. You will be able to consolidate your present knowledge by making connections between different aspects of what you know and what you do in your daily practice.

The purposes of this section are for you to:

* review your own learning

* review what you have learned about children's learning in the past

* study some articles about children's learning which may stimulate new learning for you

* consider the ways in which your understanding of learning has affected, and will, in future, affect your practice when assessing children's learning

There are four activities in this section: you are recommended to do them all, since they form a logical sequence. You may however want to return to Activity 3C, **Learning about learning,** later on in your work, if you feel you did not have time to do it justice at the time.

1 hour

ACTIVITY 3A   **Pathways of learning**

PREPARATION

Coloured felt tip pens
Large and small sheets of paper

Notes to Group Leaders

You may need to reassure diffident artists. A doodle or 'word picture' rather than a perfectly finished drawing is all that is needed. During trialling we found some groups needed a suggestion to start their own ideas flowing. Here are some examples of these:

Learning to be a group leader

Learning chemistry at school

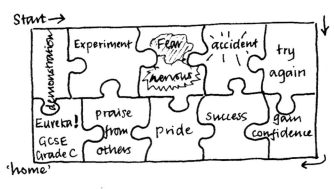

Learning with a new computer

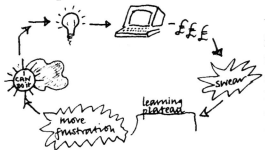

INTRODUCTION TO THE ACTIVITY

We have all experienced different kinds of learning, but it isn't always easy to talk about these differences. One way of talking about learning is to think of it as rather like travelling around the country, by different sorts of roads, by different routes, to various destinations (and sometimes in very different weather conditions). Sometimes we feel as if we're on an empty motorway, speeding towards a big city we've always wanted to visit; sometimes our learning feels more like a traffic jam in a crowded town, where we've been stuck for hours. Sometimes we feel as if we're travelling along a winding country lane, - we're not quite sure where we'll end up, but the scenery is beautiful - and we've plenty of time to stop and look at the interesting places we pass through. If you were to draw a picture or diagram of your own learning, what would it look like? Would there be motorways? dead-ends? roundabouts? blizzards? fog? breakdowns? breathtaking mountain passes?

The purposes of this activity are for you to:

• review your own learning

• think about the patterns in children's learning

ACTIVITY 3A	Pathways of Learning

1. Working on your own, use the pens and paper provided to make a picture or diagram that represents the different kinds of learning that you have experienced yourself - either as an adult or as a child. You may choose to use the metaphor of learning as a journey - or maybe your learning looks more like a merry-go-round, or an ant-hill, a carnival procession or a pilgrimage - the possibilities are endless.

   Use your picture to show all the different ways in which you learn and have learned.

2. Working in groups of four or five, discuss your pictures, looking for similarities and differences.

3. Now think about one or two of the children with whom you work. Can you see any evidence in them of these different kinds of learning? What sorts of pathways and patterns can you see in their learning, as you watch them play and interact with you and their peers?

4. Bring your discussion to close by coming together as a whole group to pull out any general points you may wish to share about differences and similarities in learning.

1 hour or longer
if you have time

| ACTIVITY 3B | Stocktaking |

PREPARATION

Copies of the Handout, or a selection of the incomplete sentences on the Handout with some additions of your own to suit your group members' needs
Flip chart sheets (to be saved for Activity 3D)
Pens and notebooks

Notes to Group Leaders

This is a long and challenging activity, since group members are being invited to look back critically at their own learning. If in the past they have been encouraged to 'learn by swallowing', they may need support in taking the daring step of comparing what they have been told with their own real life experiences.

You may need to support group members in finding the practical applications of their learning from the past as well as in identifying the least valuable elements of their learning.

As group members examine some of the concepts they were taught in the past, they will need to check whether they all understand the same thing by the words they use. For example, is a 'language deprived child' a child whose first language is not English, or a child who has not had many experiences of hearing stories read aloud, or a child who is not disposed to talk to strange adults in an unfamiliar group setting? But equally, group members will need to consider whether these concepts are beneficial or damaging to their understanding of young children's learning. For example, does this same concept 'language deprived' act as a label, suggesting that the child has a permanent language deficit? Does it suggest that the child **cannot** communicate in words? These would be good reasons for deciding not to make use of this concept in the future.

INTRODUCTION TO THE ACTIVITY

We can easily find out about the countries of origin of the stores in our food cupboard. The raisins are from Morocco, the mustard from Germany, the rice from India... But what about the mental store cupboards, where we store our learning about how children learn? Where did that learning come from? Is it still useful? Or should it be discarded?

In this activity you will be able to draw on your work in Sections One (Values) and Two (Feelings) to re-examine your own learning about children's learning, and to undertake a kind of 'stocktaking'.

The purposes of this activity are for you to:

* review what you have learned in the past about how young children learn

* identify what is valuable and of practical use to you in assessing children's learning

* discard the mouldy or outdated stores of knowledge accumulated over the years

*Making
Assessment
Work*

ACTIVITY 3B	Stocktaking

1.   Working on your own, complete the sentences on the Handout provided. If they do not apply to your previous experience or training, please feel free to alter the wording to suit yourself - or to leave them blank.

2.   Working in pairs, discuss what you have written. Look out for similarities and differences in what you have learned about learning.

3.   Working in pairs, look back over your Handout sheets and mark what you consider to be, for you, the three **most valuable** aspects of learning about learning, in your recent and distant past. Try to think of some examples in your own recent practice where you found yourself referring either openly, or privately to what you know about children's learning. In the same way, mark anything on your Handout that seems to represent some learning that has never really been of any practical value to you, or that you feel you have never put into practice.

4.   Working in groups of six or eight, summarise your work so far on a flip chart, so that everyone can see the outcomes of each pair's discussion. Try to sort your learning into categories that show where, when and how you acquired this understanding - from your training and reading, from your work experience, or from your personal experience of your own children, and whether or not this has been useful to you. You might want to divide the sheet of paper like this:

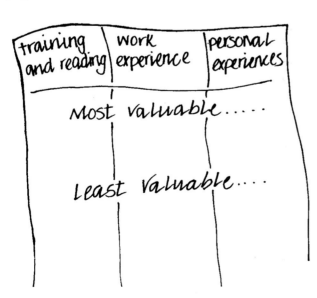

5.   Working all together, review the learning listed on the flip chart sheets. Which items in your 'mental store cupboards' are in good condition and ready to use? Which stores must be discarded? Which key ideas will inform your current observations and assessments of children's learning?

Making
Assessment
Work

LOOKING AT LEARNING

Working on your own, complete the following sentences:

1. Learning from personal experiences:

    • My grandmother/mother always used to say...

    • Now I am a parent/I have children I care deeply about, I have learned...

    • Some of my friends' children have made me think...

    • My knowledge of myself as a learner tells me...

2. Learning from your work experiences:

    • The different things I see parents do and say has taught me...

    • My first boss (early years) had a 'bee in her (his) bonnet' about...

    • The educator I work with most closely is particular about...

    • The most important thing that I do now is...

    • The educator I most admire taught me...

3. Learning from training and/or reading:

    • The most memorable lecture I ever heard was about...

    • I shall always remember being told over and over again...

    • At college during my first course we studied the theories of...
      (jot down everything you can remember)

    • The course I have been on that has made the most difference to my work was about...

    • The book/article/theory I still keep and refer to about children's learning is...

ACTIVITY 3C   Learning about learning

PREPARATION

Copies of the articles provided for discussion, so that each pair of group members has a copy of a selected article. If these articles do not seem suitable, the group leader could provide alternatives.

OHP projector or flip chart, paper and pens.

Time needed will depend on size of group - minimum is about 1 hour, and 2 hours would be the maximum at any one session

Notes to Group Leaders

This activity falls into three distinct phases. In the first, which should be a separate session, group members will work in pairs, reading their selected article, and preparing a short (about five minutes) presentation of the key ideas in the article. Encourage the pairs to use an OHP transparency or flip chart sheet to summarise a handful of points in what they have read.

The next phase is for the presentations themselves: you will need to allocate time for each pair to present their work, and make sure that time limits are strictly kept, so that every pair gets a fair hearing. Keep the flip chart sheets and transparencies for use in the next activity.

The third phase is when the whole group has the opportunity to discuss what they have heard.

Some members of the group may feel anxious about the demands of the task. If they are given enough preparation time and encouraging support, they will feel confident enough to offer their contribution to rest of the group (five minutes goes very quickly, once you get started!).

If the group is enthusiastic about this activity, once completed, they may want to follow it up by repeating the experience, this time using articles they have chosen for themselves.

INTRODUCTION TO THE ACTIVITY

In this activity you will work with a partner to read and discuss someone else's views about children's learning, and then present those ideas to the rest of the group.

The purposes of this activity are for you to:

* use the thinking of others to stimulate your own thinking

* question how what you actually do connects with what you know about children's learning

1. Working with a partner, select one of the articles provided. When you have read the article, spend some time with your partner checking it through, making sure that you both share an understanding of the author's key words and concepts.

2. Now work with your partner to prepare a short presentation on the article for the rest of the group, lasting no more than five minutes. Outline the key points (only a few headings) of the article on an OHP transparency or flip chart sheet to make it easier for your colleagues to follow your presentation. **(Note:** these two parts of the activity will take place at a session before the presentations themselves.)

3. At the session proper, the presentations will take place: a maximum of five minutes for each pair.

4. After you have listened to each presentation you may want to ask some questions of clarification ('What **exactly** does the author mean by ....?') before you move on to more general discussion.

5. In the general discussion of each article, the following questions may be useful starting points:

    •   What do we know about common patterns in children's learning?

    •   What do we know about individual differences in children's learning?

    •   In what ways do we make use of this knowledge?
        -   in our curriculum for children with special learning needs?
        -   in our provision of an early years curriculum?
        -   in our assessment practice?

    •   What connections can we make between the key ideas of these authors and what we see children do in our workplaces?

    •   What connections can we make between the key ideas of these authors and what we ourselves do as early years educators?

6. FOLLOW-UP ACTIVITY: if you have all enjoyed this activity, you may decide, as a group, to repeat it, using an article that you have found for yourself in a recent journal or magazine.

7. Keep the notes of the main points of your presentations for use in the following activity.

ACTIVITY 3C   Learning about learning

SELECTED ARTICLES

A   Drummond, M.J. (1990) 'Issues of Quality: Curriculum in the Early Years' in Pugh, G. (ed) *Quality and Equality for Under Fives. Better Access to Better Services* NES Arnold/National Children's Bureau

B   Whitehead, M. (1990) 'First Words. The language diary of a bilingual child's early speech' *Early Years.* 10, 2, Spring, TACTYC, Trentham Books, Stoke on Trent

C   Goldschmied, E. (1990) 'What to Do With the Under Twos. Heuristic Play. Infants Learning' in Rouse, D. (ed) *Babies and Toddlers: Carers and Educators. Quality for Under Threes* National Children's Bureau

D   Nutbrown, C. (1989) 'Patterns in Painting, Patterns in Play: Young Children Learning' *Topic: practical applications of research in education.* NFER NELSON

E   Armstrong, M. (1990) 'Another Way of Looking' *Forum* 33, 1, 12-16

F   Alexander, R., Rose J., and Woodhead, C . (1992) *Curriculum organisation and classroom practice in primary schools. A discussion paper. paras 107- 116.* Department of Education and Science

Group leaders may prefer to select other articles of particular interest to their group from early years journals (for example *Nursery World* or *Child Education*). It is important to choose discussion materials which are about children's learning. If the group works with babies or with primary school children then you may want to choose more articles that describe learning at that stage.

ISSUES OF QUALITY: CURRICULUM IN THE EARLY YEARS

Drummond, M,J, (1990) 'Issues of Quality: Curriculum in the Early Years'
in Pugh G (ed) *Quality and Equality for Under Fives. Better Access to Better Services*
NES Arnold/National Children's Bureau.

I have divided this paper into three unequal sections: first, some introductory remarks centred around one of the words in the conference title; secondly, some thoughts about what some selected aspects of quality might mean for young children; and thirdly, some ideas about what the process of achieving quality might mean for early years practitioners.

THE IMPORTANCE OF "AND"

I will begin by reflecting on the sometimes contrary feeling that comes over me when I read lists of benchmarks of quality. For every golden word I read on these lists - like stability, or equality, or co-operation, or autonomy - I want to add another word that ever so slightly undermines the first. Let's take, for example, equality, a concept that no-one can quarrel with as it stands; and yet I do worry about what the concept of equality might exclude. Might it mean that every child has to have the same curriculum? Might equality drive out difference? I want to stand for equality *and* difference. And similarly with stability. I can see the importance of stability, keeping the boundaries safe, having clear expectations, knowing they'll be met; but again I want to add something else - the idea of challenge. It is possible that stability may sometimes be the enemy of challenge, and so I want to couple the two concepts together: stability *and* challenge.

Another example: sociability, friendships, good relationships in the peer group - all important aspects of quality. *And* I believe it's important to leave space in the curriculum for privacy, not for loneliness, but for being alone. Early years settings are crowded places, but individuals have the right, I believe, to get out of a crowd, even at three years old. A rug over a table, a den for one, is a valuable item in our provision.

We talk a good deal about the concept of relevance, the importance of building on children's past experience, helping them to make connections between what they already know and what they will learn next. Relevance,

yes - *and* brand new experiences too, that haven't had preparatory stages. What could possibly prepare a young child for seeing an elephant?

Another important pair of words linked by *and*: reality and fantasy. One of the most exciting books I've read this year is Kieran Egan's *Primary Understanding* (1988). Egan argues that one of the things we know about children's thinking is that: "a prominent part of their mental life is fantasy, and that much of this fantasy is playful and energetic, an important and wholesome activity." (p13)

But, he goes on, this obvious intellectual strength of children has been woefully neglected and depreciated by educationalists. Some of the blame for this rests with Dewey, whose emphasis on the learner's previous experience has been, according to Egan, widely misinterpreted.

"Experience" has come to be seen largely in terms of the everyday practical world of children's lives. Dewey's work has tended to focus attention on "the mundane and practical world in which children live." What has been lost is the ability to see that world as the child sees it "transfigured by fantasy" (p20). Egan argues that we do wrong to neglect this world: "The child who cannot on the one side, conserve liquid quantity, may, on the other, lead a vivid intellectual life, brimming with knights, dragons, witches and star warriors." (p23)

When children play with smurfs, and will break off for lunch only with reluctance and after terrible threats, it is not because smurfs are part of their everyday reality. But the children, in their play, have been dealing with concepts that are real to them: good and bad, big and little, brave and cowardly, oppressors and oppressed, safety and danger. Egan argues we can only engage reality in curriculum if we start through what children know best - the reality of fantasy, the most profound and fundamental concepts of love, hate, joy, fear, power, hope and disappointment.

There are plenty more characteristics of quality that can be linked with the word *and*: independence *and* dependence; success *and* failure; joy *and* sorrow; personal *and* impersonal; safety *and* danger; hygiene *and* mud. But now I want to move on, and examine three aspects of a quality curriculum in more detail, thinking about what they might mean in practice for the children on the receiving end of them.

ASPECTS OF QUALITY

First let's look at the second item on the list in the conference paper contributed by Balaguer and Penn: a *quality environment*. The authors suggest a number of questions we might ask about the environment we provide, to which I want to add some more, which cluster around the concept of ownership. I want to ask: whose environment is it? By whose perspective do we evaluate it? Through whose eyes do we look at it? What sort of debate are we going to have about it? Who is going to be involved in the debate? And who excluded? I sometimes wonder if our working environments are designed with the adults' priorities in mind, rather than the children's. Our priorities are defensible, of course: a clean sink is better than a mucky one. But only if it can be mucky some of the time.

Or we can take another aspect of the quality environment: safety. Of course the environment has to be safe. But not too safe. Do we provide opportunities for working with wood? Are hammers safe? Are chisels safe? Or saws? When we think of the rules and regulations in force in settings for young children, it is very clear that many of them are justified in terms of safety. And I believe that many of them are also the expression of our own fears and anxieties - and that certainly some of them are historical records of recent accidents in the workplace. There's a balance to be drawn between wrapping babies up at birth in cotton wool, and sending toddlers out to play on the motorway. We need to make sure we evaluate safety from the children's perspective and not solely on the basis of our own emotions. If saws are acceptable, what about trees? Is a three year old entitled to climb a tree? Fall out of a tree? Or what about mud? Is mud dangerous? The routine at meal-times is another whole area of this general debate: who sets the standards by which this aspect of quality is to be evaluated? Who sets the seal of approval or disapproval on eating with a spoon? Or with your fingers?
I know - we all know - where young children stand on mud, and trees, and eating with their fingers. I don't believe we will lose out on quality if we hand some of the decisions about their environment over to the children.

The second aspect of quality that I will examine comes up as the third on Helen Penn's list: *quality learning experiences*. Here my questions, once again, start with a question of ownership: whose learning is it? Of course, we know it is the children's learning, but we keep a very tight hold on it for all that; and sometimes we miss completely what it is that children are learning because we are so entranced with what we want them to learn.

I am, generally, optimistic about this area of our work. We know a good deal about how children learn, how they actively create meaning for themselves from a welter of first hand experiences, mediated and reflected on through language. We know our children as active learners, we know we cannot do their learning for them. And sometimes there are moments when we see young children learning in this way before our very eyes: moments when children take command of their learning, restructuring their worlds, their meanings, and their understandings, freely and creatively. But these moments do not necessarily happen every half hour - or even every day. And sometimes this is because we don't let them happen: we've got minibeasts to do - or our topic on transport - or our Mother's Day cards.

The last aspect of quality that I will consider is the seventh on your list: *valuing diversity*, which includes, I believe, the need to respect, and build on, individual differences. This is an aspect of quality that we tend to pride ourselves on: the rhetoric of the unique individual is one of the self-evident truths of the early years worker. And yet institutional settings, however informal, are not designed for individuals, but for crowds. And the mentality of crowd control does creep into our work. I have spent some time observing four year old children in their first few weeks of school, and I have been enormously struck by the effort that goes into establishing the concepts of "all" and "everyone". "All" and "everyone" are words heard in classrooms far more often than 'diversity'. Or 'some of you', or 'two of you', or 'one of you'. Much as we may relish the concept of individual difference and diversity, we may find it very hard to take in practice; we certainly work very hard to establish conformity as a baseline expectation.

I have become more concerned about this issue over the last eighteen months or so, as the current anxiety about baseline assessment reaches panic proportions. I have seen dozens of instruments for baseline assessment, all of which were drawn up with the very best of intentions, but many of which emphasise conformity, normality, sameness, the model pupil. None of them start with the words: What's different about this child? Not many of these instruments are as dangerously misconceived as one I have seen which applies a strictly numerical six point scale to a selection of attributes (including toilet training) - no verbal descriptions are given. But the very idea of trying to capture the richness of the individual spirit on one side of A4, ruled up into pre-determined categories, is deeply antithetical to the concept of diversity.

ACHIEVING QUALITY

In this concluding section, I will consider some of the tasks we might profitably set ourselves, if our curriculum of quality is not to remain a list of golden words on a page.

First, I believe, we must redistribute the time that we spend on the complementary activities of planning and reviewing the curriculum. At the moment, the early years practitioners I know best, teachers in nursery and primary classes, are under tremendous pressure to improve their planning. But planning, important though it is, is always about what we would like to happen, the world as I mean it to be when I'm lying in bed in the morning (and it includes fine weather and international nuclear disarmament). Review is a more demanding process, more concentrated, more closely connected to reality. In this diagram (opposite) I have tried to summarise some of the characteristics of the two processes, showing how, although we cannot, of course, dispense with planning, we must make certain that the time we spend on it doesn't squeeze out the more important business of review.

PLAN OR REVIEW

looking ahead	or	looking back
good intentions	or	what actually happened
"Wouldn't it be lovely..."	or	"Well, was it?"
wishful thinking	or	factual descriptions
aspirations	or	analysis
theories	or	evidence
hope for the best	or	real understanding

A second part of the challenging process of achieving quality will involve giving up some of our professional defensiveness, and learning to listen to other people, even when we have no reason for welcoming what they are going to say. When parents talk to practitioners, the parents may see why they have to say as positive, constructive, supportive (as I know from my own experience as a parent). But those very same words may be experienced by the practitioner (and here I speak as a teacher) as destructive, critical and unsupportive: my professional defensiveness leaps to my rescue when parents find fault with my work. It's very difficult to look a parent in the eye and say: ... 'yes, that's a good point, we'll certainly have to think about it.' Or rather, it's easy, if you think the parent has got a good point, one with which you agree. But what if you don't agree? We all like to hear about what we do well - can we genuinely welcome the chance to hear about what we do less well?

A third requirement of the process will be asking ourselves questions about our curriculum - and not just 'what' and 'how' questions, which are relatively easy, comfortable, reassuring. Asking each other 'why' questions is a more challenging process, and - given that we share a common culture - unlikely to happen, unless we make strenuous efforts to break the rules of polite society, and persistently ask each other the questions that don't normally get asked. A fascinating book, *Pre-school in Three Cultures* (Tobin et al, 1989), has recently illustrated for me the power of the unexpected question. The authors describe how groups of pre-school workers from Japan, China and the United States were brought together to discuss video tapes made in their workplaces. The Japanese kindergarten teacher is asked 'What kind of child are you trying to produce in your pre-school?' and replies 'a child-like child'.

And so, of course, the next question has to be: and what *is* a child-like child?

What a question! But what a world of understanding might open up if we were to ask it - and others like it.

Another element in the difficult, but not impossible, process of achieving quality, will involve learning something about ourselves and our emotional stability and flexibility. We all know that the early years curriculum is not simply a matter of cognitive development. We would all hope to be sensitive to our children's pressing affective concerns, as well as the intellectual pursuits they are engaged in. But our own emotional set, our own upbringing, our training as little children, may get in the way of achieving quality in this domain. I was brought up to hide many of my feelings: I was taught not to express boredom on a long car journey, or jealousy of my younger brother, or distress over a broken toy, or anger at my parents' use of authority. I was taught to be very wary of all those negative emotions in myself and others. Many of you will also have been educated in this way, and the result is that when we come face to face with anger, sorrow or fear, we do our best to dispose of it, show it the door, pass the kleenex. This attitude will not be helpful to us in our work with young children if we are to work towards a curriculum that is rich in emotional content as well as intellectual challenge. Our impulse to deny strong and difficult feelings in ourselves may need some critical attention if we are not to deny our children a full and complex emotional life.

My last suggestion for achieving quality is also concerned with ourselves, the practitioners responsible for quality. I believe that we have got to learn to behave in ways that many of us may find difficult - again, because of our own upbringing. I believe that the corny old adage - 'little children should be seen and not heard' - may have come to be closely associated with those who work with young children. Do we, too, choose to be seen, but not heard? Can we break out of our elected silence, and learn to be noisier about our work, our achievements, and our vision of a quality curriculum for all young children?

Here I'd like to borrow a powerful concept from the social anthropologist Edwin Ardener, who has explored the idea of 'muted groups' in society. Building on contemporary feminist theory, Ardener argues that in many of the studies of traditional societies written by anthropologists, the women of the society have not been given the opportunity to express their understandings, their meanings. The symbolic weight of female models of society remains unexpressed, silent, muted. The muted group does not form part of the dominant communicative system of the society.

There are parallels here, I believe, for all those who work with the youngest children in our society. Early years practitioners frequently express an awareness of what Ardener would label their mutedness. Cynthia James, until recently Inspector for Early Years in the London Borough of Haringey, put it recently like this: 'We are women, they are little children. We make a noise, but we are not heard'. I believe that none of us can afford to endure this condition of mutedness any longer. We must become noisier and more articulate, seen and heard, and, more importantly, understood.

REFERENCES

Ardener, E. (1975) 'Belief and the problem of women' in Ardener, S. (ed.) *Perceiving Women* Dent

Egan, K. (1988) *Primary Understanding* Routledge

Tobin, J.J., Wu, D. & Davidson, D. (1989) *Pre-School in Three Cultures* Yale University Press

LOOKING AT LEARNING

FIRST WORDS -
THE LANGUAGE DIARY OF A BILINGUAL CHILD'S EARLY SPEECH

Whitehead, M. (1990)
'First Words The language diary of a bilingual child's early speech'
Early Years. 10, 2, Spring, TACTYC Trentham Books

'A word is a microcosm of human consciousness'
Vygotsky (1986)

Children's first single words and word combinations reflect the social experiences and meanings central to their lives. Much of this early language is about the 'here and now' world of significant people, actions, food, the body, clothes, animals, vehicles, toys, games, household objects and social conventions. Other important categories are location: the 'up', 'down' and 'under' of toddlers' talk, as well as adjectives, and those sounds, words and gestures which point things out. All these themes are of considerable social and cultural significance because they function like commentaries on the traditions, attitudes and rituals of the home and community in which the young speaker is developing.

The following account of my grand-daughter's first words demonstrates the uniqueness of early language acquisition: every child's infancy, upbringing and socio-cultural situation is different. N lives in Israel with her English mother and her Israeli father whose first language is Hebrew. During the period of the diary the household also included her paternal grandparents who spoke Hebrew in their social and professional circles but frequently used German in their personal and domestic life.

Their origins were Austro-Hungarian and Hungarian frequently surfaced as the language of reminiscences and of traditional songs, nursery rhymes and games with baby N. N was regularly cared for by these grandparents who used English as well as Hebrew in their interactions with her. N's parents decided to introduce English as her first language, mainly because the extended family, neighbourhood and eventual pre-school provision would be almost totally Hebrew speaking. This approach is generally known as successive bilingualism (Arnberg 1987), but it is important to note that in this case words from the second language appear very early in the diary, at fourteen

months. This confirms the view that young bilinguals do begin by building up a vocabulary of words from both languages (Crystal 1987). In this particular study the special advantages and experience of a bilingual household and the effects of a notable input from picture books, reading and story telling are obvious. N's first word was 'book' and it was used as a request for her daily sessions of reading which involved sitting on the couch with an adult and a pile of favourite picture books and sharing in pointing, naming and listening to stories. The immense advantages of such an early acquaintance with narratives, pictures and listening to written language forms have been noted by Wells (1986) and linked with rapid language development and early insights into the nature of literacy.

Researchers who have a particularly close relationship with their young subjects have also identified ways in which the characters and events encountered in books and oral story telling enrich and extend the child's understanding of people and the world (Butler 1979, Payton 1984).

THE FIRST THREE MONTHS

A table of N's first thirty words, spanning three months, is presented at the end of this account. A glance at this table indicates that N's first words are about her family life, daily routines and possessions and reflect her considerable skill in directing adults and gaining their co-operation. Such fields of meaning appear to be of primary significance in most studies of monolingual and bilingual infants. That important first word, 'book', was used initially in an extended way to refer to all the written and pictorial material which the family read. In the month that followed N produced the conventional words and gesture of farewell and then the greeting, 'hallo'. This expression has special significance in a household where international telephone calls, as well as local calls, are the frequent and valued means of linking a widely dispersed family. N soon began to use 'hallo' for real telephone greetings, as well as saying it into her toy telephone. The term 'gone' emerges as a very early comment on finishing food and drink; two months later it is combined with 'Dada' as a comment on his leaving for work. The term remains a useful part of this child's vocabulary, reflecting her general realisation that people, objects and materials come and go in the environment. This first month of words, seven items in all, ends with the conventional naming of mother and father and the word for a favourite daily routine, 'bath'.

The second month added five new lexical terms to N's repertoire, starting with an apparent comment on a fascinating bodily function which cannot be ignored and causes quite a stir among the adult carers! Food is now marked out by a word for a specific favourite, 'apple', as well as an interesting example of word invention. The term 'hum-hum' seems to be based on the form 'yum-yum', sometimes used playfully by her parents to encourage the eating up of food, but it was soon generalised over a wide area by N. She said it very excitedly whenever food was being prepared or eaten, and by the time she was fourteen months old she used it both to identify and to demand special favourites, such as olives and cakes. It also became her general term for any meal. This month produced a linguistic reference to the games of peekaboo played with her father using German expressions. German is a third language used in the family and 'cuck-oo' is N's approximation of 'guck-guck'. She appeared to use the term primarily as an invitation to adults to play with her, although she also used it as part of the game's format. The English equivalent, 'boo', mainly used by N's mother, emerged six weeks later. At the end of this period the little girl utters her first direct and unmistakeable instruction, 'up'. From the start it was not only used as a request to be lifted up, or out of a push-chair or high-chair; it was also an indicator for 'down', as in 'put me down' and 'take me downstairs'. It was further extended almost immediately to become a comment on changes in the location of objects in space, functioning as linguistic marker for dropped objects and things actually in the process of falling.

In the third month N's new word additions accelerated to eighteen and this included some important new developments. First came the valuable 'no' which was to be followed by the affirmative two weeks later. A special member of the household, the family cat, is labelled by the generic term 'cat' but will not be called 'Sam' for another two months. A set of playthings which are very important to N are labelled in the period, starting with a small toy dog which goes everywhere with her, is her crucial comforter in times of distress, and quite essential when she is settling down to sleep. Young children's deep attachments to such chosen comforters are well documented in psychoanalytic studies of child development (Winnicott, 1971), as well as being known to many families. N also used her word for this toy dog to refer to real dogs and eventually, dogs in picture books. The word 'keys' is more than an object label for N: bunches of house and car keys were among her first favourite toys and her demands for them were very insistent. She would quickly acquire any which were put down within her reach and refuse to give them up. She could also be distracted from anger or distress by being given a bunch of keys to jangle. Another favourite game was chasing a rolling 'ball' and this term is also in the early words collection. This third month of words includes a second food item, 'crackers', and the family 'car' which she apparently associated with outings and with significant people coming and going. The daily routines of dressing began to be commented on: perhaps the 'socks' and 'shoes' come first because of their close association in her life with getting ready to go out. Hats delighted and fascinated her and throughout the hot summer months in her home country she always had to wear a sun-hat, as did many of the adults she knew. The use of 'hat' became extended a month later to refer to her own hair and then to other people's hair, particularly if it was thick and curly and might perhaps suggest the appearance and texture of a hat. An interesting example of an adjective occurs towards the end of this period when N takes up the term 'hot' which was used by her family as a very serious warning to stop her touching the oven door when it was in use. She initially said it herself, with an obvious sense of fear, to refer to the oven and then extended it, with similarly expressive caution, to cups of coffee which were also hot and a danger to her.

Perhaps the most interesting new addition in this month of words is a set of no less than four instructions. Suddenly N is able to signal linguistically her requests for adult help and can say 'come', 'walk', 'push' and 'out'. Typically, for this energetic infant living in an out-of-doors Mediterranean culture, these instructions refer to pushing back patio doors, pushing a push-chair and asking adults to come and take her out for a walk.

To summarise these first three months of word acquisitions: approximately eighteen of the thirty function as naming and commenting activities about such topics as people, foods, toys, animals, clothes, and smells. Ideas of absence and danger are also labelled. The usefulness of these naming and commenting words is their flexibility for the young child's purposes when she has only a limited vocabulary. Labels can be used as requests in a familiar, shared, social context. For example, 'apple' or 'cracker' can be said in such a way and in such circumstances that it conveys the meaning, 'I want an apple', or a 'cracker'. Context, plus the appropriate intonation in the voice can turn a label into a question: 'cat', where is the cat? N's use of 'hot' often appeared to be a request for information: is the oven hot, can I go near the oven door? The power of commands and instructions has been mentioned and N was using five such items by the end of this period. Six examples of social responses and games are recorded here, namely 'bye-bye', 'hallo', 'guck-guck', 'no', 'yes', 'boo'. They reflect the young child's integration into family life, as well as her ability to influence others, cooperate with them and express her own desires. There is one recorded example of a word category which was very broad or generalised: 'book' was used for all papers, books and documents looked at, but this was narrowed down in the following months. Several words start as personal and specific references but they are quickly pressed into wider use, as with the toy dog and hat examples, and 'yum-yum' for favourite foods, meals and the general eating and preparation of foods in the household. Research suggests that children's early meanings appear to evolve gradually to take over the conventional and agreed meaning of their language community, or communities, through these strategies of over-extension (book = all readable material) and under-extension (dog = my toy comforter). Many personal and inexplicable associations or mismatches also occur in this unique process of learning how to mean (Halliday 1975) by trial and error. This collection is also full of instances of early simplified pronunciation: the omission of initial consonants in 'ock' (sock), 'es' (yes) and 'at' (hat). The omission of final consonants occurs in 'boo' (book) and 'do-do' (doggy) and

there are several simplifications of complex clusters and sound patterns: 'a-pa' (apple), 'ka-ka' (cracker) and 'atoo' (out). These early stages of mastering a language's phonological system can be found in examples from many children in their second year (De Villiers 1979, Arnberg 1987, Crystal 1987).

THE FOURTH TO SEVENTH MONTH

N's words were collected as a language diary until she was nearly eighteen months old, by which time there were too many new words to itemise and two, three and four word combinations were coming thick and fast! Her language development was then recorded by regular audio-taping sessions. A summary of the main achievements of these months, 1:02 to 1:05, can only give a brief indication of the speed and originality of N's early language and speech development, but it is not untypical of the achievements of many other children (see References). In the fourth month of the diary the new words accelerated to sixty-four, a large increase compared with the previous month's eighteen words. As her vocabulary increases, so do the instances of simplified pronunciations of the many phonetically complex words she is tackling, for example, 'poon' (spoon), 'pane' (plane), 'bed' (bread) and 'douser' (trousers). Names for parts of the body and for household items and activities predominate, but there is a considerable number of words for animals seen in books and labelled in her daily reading sessions. Two-word combinations such as 'bye-bye Dada' and 'bye-bye cat' appear, plus a delightful and certainly unimitated comment when her trousers were taken off, 'gone douser'. Linguists identify these unique kinds of unimitated combinations as the first examples of grammatical sentences. The words are ordered in ways which clearly convey meanings and are initially focused on actions, possessions, locations and labelling (De Villiers & De Villiers 1979) and, as in N's first productions, ideas of non-existence or absence.

N is the child of a bilingual family and in this month two words of her second language are used for the first time. One is a command addressed to the cat, 'boy' (Hebrew for 'come') and the second, 'agala', refers to her favourite forms of transport: the push-chair and supermarket trolleys. The Hebrew word 'agala' does conventionally refer to both of them, as well as to most other types of trolley, and N later applies this useful word to her large elephant toy which also runs on wheels. During this period some very expressive and musical language developments were apparent: a prolonged 'aah' sound was regularly used when she was cuddling people and toys very affectionately. Singing, accompanied by head shaking and swinging her legs or tapping her feet, was a rhythmic and distinctive 'la-la-la' sound. This seemed to occur most frequently and spontaneously when N was being taken for walks in her pushchair and could thump the foot-rest and sides energetically.

In the fifth month, when N was fifteen months old, her new words increased again with eighty-nine additions and included the first names of her parents, her first version of her own name, and the names of grandparents and family friends. Two large categories of words now stand out: the names of animals and people, and words about the world outside the house. The size and significance of this latter group may be a reflection of the family's outdoor life-style in the Mediterranean early summer. The category has in it such items as 'flas' (flowers), 'by' (fly, insect, butterfly), 'san' (sand), 'tee' (tree). Second language words increase suddenly to twelve items and include the first lines of a favourite Hebrew nursery rhyme, the overheard command to a dog to 'come here' as well as the Hebrew words for 'bottom', 'car' and 'grandad'. A significant linguistic newcomer in English is the possessive pronoun 'mine', first said as she clutched a special piece of drawing paper. There is also an interesting cluster of further two-word combinations, ranging from the conventional greetings, 'hallo Dada' and 'hallo do-do', to more unusual creations. These include, 'out cat' (the cat wants to go out), 'no agala' (I don't want to go in the pushchair), 'more tortoise' (I want to see another tortoise), and 'more sea' (I want to go to the sea again).

This small girl's rapid progress in gaining a hold on her first languages is demonstrated in the six months of the data collection when her additional new vocabulary items total an impressive one hundred and thirty-three. This includes a group of basic Hebrew words, instructions and nursery songs and a noticeable preference for some Hebrew terms, although she knows their English equivalents.

Perhaps this is the first example in the diary of one of the major advantages of bilingualism: 'bilingual children become conscious at a much earlier age of the fact that names are arbitrarily assigned to objects and are subject to change' (Saunders 1988, p.17). This early awareness of the arbitrariness of language, that a word is a conventional sign in a particular language community and not an attribute of the thing it names, may enable young bilinguals to think more effectively with the meanings which words encode. The English 'hat' has been replaced by the Hebrew 'kova' and 'plane' gives way to 'aviron'. It may be that ease of articulation also accounts for some of these language choices. At the same time N's increasing knowledge of many English songs and nursery rhymes added new ranges to her vocabulary: fox, little lamb, baa-baa (as in Black Sheep) and 'tee-dum' (Humpty Dumpty). There is a noticeable increase in far more sophisticated English food names, for example, 'peat' (peach), 'see-ol' (cereal), 'ato' (tomato), 'corshet' (courgette), 'ashum' (mushroom) and 'durbis' (strawberries). But the real power of language to get things done in the world and to comment on events is reflected in the verbal instructions and word combinations which appear. Halliday (1975) identified these two potent language functions as the major strategies to emerge in his own son's early language development and refers to them as the pragmatic, for getting things done, and the mathetic, for commenting on the world. N's instructions include 'come on', 'get it', 'wash it', 'cut it', 'cose it' (close it) and the delightful four word phrase, 'dirty hand wash it'. Comments range from 'teddy ball' (teddy has a ball) and 'coffee Dada' (coffee for Daddy), to 'gasses on nose' (glasses on nose), and the appropriately used imitation of her father's exclamation, 'Oh gosh'! In the final weeks of this diary N was visiting her maternal grandparents in the UK and the change of environment and culture added many new words to her repertoire, for examples, 'quirrel' (squirrel) and 'ano' (piano). She also began to comment quietly to herself about what she was doing, as in 'sitting down', or 'writing', and was overheard, while playing alone, repeating softly the opening lines of a nursery rhyme,

'rat tat tat
who is that
only ganma .... cat'

Although size of vocabulary is only one element in language comprehension and production it would appear that the study's total word count of 316 is very high for a 16 months child. Crystal (1987, p.42) suggests a rough estimate of about fifty words in use at 18 months and probably five times as many understood. Perhaps we can surmise that N's rapid language development had been accelerated by the bi- and multilingual home setting, the rich diversity of her early book sharing experiences, and the conversations she participated in with her adult carers.

CONCLUSION

This diary study has revealed some of the ways in which one young child was learning to label and comment on her world and gain the help and interest of her carers. It also suggests that encounters with the poetry and narrative forms of two cultures were being used at a remarkably early age in order to reflect upon personal experiences and make sense of them. The actual collection and analysis of N's first words has been, like her language learning, a truly family affair. This has confirmed for us our generally held assumption that there are unique opportunities and insights available to those who attempt to study the language developments of their own children and grandchildren (see Halliday 1975, Butler 1979, De Villiers 1979, Payton 1984, Saunders 1988). There is an opposing tradition, of course, which claims that a very close involvement with one's human sources and data produces a subjective blurring of perception and judgement. However, modern research and common human experience suggest that language studies, particularly of early language acquisition, need a richly detailed and shared background of knowledge about community, cultural traditions, homes, relationships, private events and affective responses (for example, Heath 1983, Wells 1986). This insight was expressed and developed many years ago in the work of Vygotsky:

"To understand another's speech, it is not sufficient to understand his words - we must understand his thought. But even that is not enough - we must also know its motivation" (1986, p.253).

The implication for professional carers and teachers of young children is clear: if we are to study, understand and even assess the language achievements of young children, we must as far as possible be true partners and sharers in their worlds.

NOTES

1. I am deeply grateful to Dr Dulcie Engel for collecting her daughter's first words so efficiently and sensitively and allowing me to use the material in this way.

2. As this is an informal study I have not used a phonetic alphabet but simply reproduced the child's words as they sounded to an English speaker. Only the first three months of the data are tabulated and discussed in detail.

LEXICAL ITEMS

Diary Months	Age	Number
First Three	0:10-1:01	30
Fourth	1:02	64
Fifth	1:03	89
Sixth	1:04	133
Total for Six Months		316

REFERENCES

Arnberg, L. (1987) *Raising Children Bilingually: The Pre-School Years*, Multilingual Matters, Clevedon

Butler, D. (1979) *Cushla and Her Books*, Hodder & Stoughton, Sevenoaks

Crystal, D. (1987) *The Cambridge Encyclopedia of Language*, Cambridge University Press

De Villiers, P.A. and De Villiers, J.G. (1979) *Early Language*, Fontana, London.

Halliday M.A.K. (1975) *Learning How to Mean. Explorations in the development of Language*, Arnold, London.

Heath, S.B. (1983) *Ways with Words Language, Life and Work in Communities and Classrooms*, Cambridge University Press.

Payton, S. (1984) 'Developing awareness of print. A young child's first steps toward literacy', *Education Review* Offset Publication, No.2, University of Birmingham.

Saunders, G. (1988) *Bilingual Children. From Birth to Teens* Multilingual Matters, Clevedon.

Vygotsky, L.S. (1986) *Thought and Language* MIT, Cambridge Mass., (Revised and edited by A. Kozulin).

Wells, G. (1986) *The Meaning Makers. Children Learning Language and Using Language to Learn* Hodder & Stoughton, London.

Winnicott, D.W. (1971) *Playing and Reality* Penguin, Harmondsworth.

First Words: the first three months			
Age	**Child word**	**Standard form**	**Comment**
0:10	boo	book	applies to books, newspapers and pictures
0:10	ba-ba	bye-bye	accompanied by waving telephone greetings (real and toy)
0:10	alo	hallo	
0:11	go	gone	food, drink finished
0:11	ma-ma	Mummy	
0:11	da-da	Daddy	
0:11	ba	bath	
0:11	poo		
1:00	hum-hum	yum-yum	demand for food and comment on its preparation
1:00	a-pa	apple	
1:00	cuck-oo	guck-guck	German for 'peekaboo'
1:00	up	up	lifting up and down and other changes of position (including dropped objects)
1:00	do	no	
1:01	ga	cat	
1:01	es	yes	
1:01	ga	car	
1:01	Dada gone		
1:01	do-do	doggy	for toy used as comforter and real dogs
1:01	come		
1:01	ock	sock(s)	
1:01	keys		
1:01	choo	shoes(s)	
1:01	boo		in conjunction with cuck-oo
1:01	at	hat	
1:01	awk	walk	
1:01	bo	ball	
1:01	push		
1:01	ot	hot	for oven door, coffee
1:01	ka-ka	cracker	
1:01	atoo	out	wants to go outside

WHAT TO DO WITH THE UNDER TWOS. HEURISTIC PLAY. INFANTS LEARNING

C
Goldschmied, E. (1990)
'What to do with the under twos. Heuristic Play. Infants Learning' in Rouse, D. (ed.) *Babies and toddlers: Carers and Educators. Quality for Under Threes* National Children's Bureau

Increasing mobility is a central factor in much that a child is able to do in the second year of his or her life. Often, of course, a child is quite mobile before her first birthday, but the term 'the second year of life' is used to describe a period when particular kinds of development go on. One aspect of this activity I have named Heuristic Play, where it will be noted that the term 'toy' is never used, only 'object'. It is described in some detail below.

The lack of understanding of the mobile child's drive to discover and learn, and the problems that this creates in a family context lie behind my use of the word 'heuristic'. This word draws attention to the significance of what the child is doing, giving the activity dignity and appreciation.

This newly acquired skill in moving is practised ceaselessly throughout a child's waking day, and it is often this passion for moving about which creates anxieties for the adults who are responsible for her. At home, in the space that a child shares with her adults, problems arise when we think of the number of times that we have to say, 'No, don't touch!', when she wants to grab and handle our most precious or dangerous (for her) objects. There is often a source of conflict when she wants to use her, now, high level precision of eye-hand-object coordination combined with her lively curiousity. If at home an active child of this age can be difficult to cope with from this point of view, the situation at the nursery is different because the adults do not live there. The needs of active young children can be handled well and the space available can be organised so as to offer interest and satisfaction.

MOBILITY BRINGS A DIFFERENCE

It is often said that the concentration we observe in the infant seated at the 'Treasure Basket' is lost when she can move about (Goldschmied 1987). Staff comment that then 'she flits from one thing to another' and that the play material available 'does not hold her attention for more than a few minutes'. Staff note that she seems to want to throw things, like the ubiquitous puzzles, on the floor, and is not interested in putting pegs in their 'proper' holes. She is, in fact saying to us, 'I'm not interested in playing with these toys *yet*, there are other things I want to do first!'. Her level of competence cannot be satisfied by this didactic play material.

Studying the play equipment we generally offer to a child in her second year, it becomes clear that there is a big gap in what we provide, and what the child finds satisfying, in her urge to explore and discover for herself the way that objects behave in space as she manipulates them. She needs a wide variety of objects with which to do this kind of experimentation, objects which are constantly new and interesting, which certainly cannot be bought from any toy catalogue.

Watching children of this age brings to mind the ancient story of Archimedes in his bath, who, when he discovered the law of the displacement of water due to the volume of his body, is said to have cried exultantly, 'Eureka, I have found it!'. The Greek word 'eurisko' means 'serves to discover or reach understanding of'. This is exactly what a young child is doing spontaneously, without any direction from adults, provided she has the materials with which to pursue her explorations. Seated at the Treasure Basket, we can imagine that she is saying, 'What is this?', but her exploration of an object has precise limits. If a ball or tin slips from her grasp and rolls away, she can follow it with her eyes but cannot move herself to retrieve it. This is a frustration which she has to tolerate, which will only be resolved (unless an attentive adult hands it back to her) when she achieves mobility through crawling and first walking.

The manipulative skill which she has acquired at an earlier stage with objects such as those in the Treasure Basket, is integrated into a successive phase, made possible by her ability to move and so take the initiative and experiment with objects in her immediate surroundings. Now we can imagine her saying, as she goes to pick up an object, 'What can I *do* with it?'

Rather than losing her ability to concentrate it becomes clear that she develops it in a direct way. It is this kind of exploratory activity which I have named 'Heuristic Play', stemming from the word 'eurisko', which has been explained above.

HOW TO PROVIDE FOR HEURISTIC PLAY

What then exactly does heuristic play consist of? In what way is it different from the range of the other activities we offer to the children? How is it organised, and what part do the adults play?

In a number of day nurseries in England, Italy and Barcelona this type of play has begun to be developed with young children up to the age of two. Detailed observations and a number of videos have been made. All the practical details given in this paper are based on the experience gained in varied settings.

The children's absorption is predominantly for putting objects in and out, filling and emptying containers and receptacles of all kinds. This develops into seeing which ones will fit into each other and which will not, for example, slipping the lengths of chain or the pom-poms into cylinders so that they pop out the other end. Here the question of success or failure does not enter in. It is all new discovery and there is no 'right' or 'wrong'. The child learns from observing directly what these objects will 'do' or 'not do' in sharp contrast to much of the 'educational' equipment which has a result predetermined by the design which has been devised by the adult maker. As has been noted above, this type of play material has its interest when some understanding of spatial relations has been acquired by the child, at a previous stage to that at which heuristic play belongs.

In going on to placing and piling, pairing and matching, selecting and discarding and noting differences and similarities, we observe a notable degree of concentration and of mental activity generated by the child herself in the secure presence of her trusted adult. She is acquiring the 'tools for learning' so fully developed by Dr. Geoffrey Waldon (Stroh and Robinson 1991). In a way, this kind of activity

is not particularly new. We have all seen children doing it, but I would say, in spite of us and not because of us. The difference is that we should recognise and cater for this type of play during some part of the nursery day. Given that the children, in many instances, spend very long hours in the nursery and may have home conditions which can offer little scope for exploratory play, it is important to ensure that this phase of their development is imaginatively provided for. The length of time that children have been observed concentrating on playing with these objects lasts for half an hour and more, developing a kind of 'one-thing-leads-to-another' logic in a pleasurable process of discovery.

MATERIAL REQUIRED

Many of the objects can be collected from home or from the nursery kitchen and a few items made by the staff themselves. Otherwise, they can be bought from an ironmonger, domestic equipment store, or knick-knack and haberdashery departments. One part of the adults' role is to collect, buy or make a good quantity of all the items listed below and to provide separate bags in which these different items should be kept when they are not in use. Parents, staff and friends can collect empty tins and jar caps of metal; woollen pom-poms can be made; wooden clothes pegs, wooden and metal curtain rings and ping-pong balls can be bought. It is also the task of the adults to search continually, with an imaginative eye, for different and suitable objects to add to the bag collection. Many of the items are similar to those included singly in the Treasure Basket, of differing size, weight, colour and texture. The items to be bought are normally used by adults, so that they will last if properly cared for, and they involve minimum expense. The underlying idea is that these objects should offer the widest variety and that they should be available to the children in large quantities.

LIST OF SUGGESTED OBJECTS:

Items for at least fifteen bags should be planned for, but the adults should seek for further objects all the time. Amounts must be generous, for example, 50 pom-poms, 60 curtain rings and pegs, and so on, which reduces any need to share and consequently occasions for conflict. If conflicts occur, the adults should examine why their intervention becomes necessary, and seek a remedy.

TO COLLECT OR MAKE

Woollen pom-poms: not too big, bright primary colours are best; cardboard cylinders of all kinds: insides of toilet rolls, computer rolls, and so on; ribbons of velvet, silk and lace; off-cuts from a carpenter; used keys; metal tops to jars; large chestnuts; bottle corks; pine cones; tins and containers of all sizes; small baskets, essential for 'filling and emptying' activities.

TO BUY

Curtain rings, wooden and metal; wooden laundry pegs; hair curlers of differing diameter; ping-pong balls; large and small corks; rubber door stops; varied lengths of chain: fine to medium sized links, not large chains; large bone buttons.

HOW AND WHEN TO INTRODUCE A HEURISTIC PLAY SESSION

Experience has shown that in providing for this kind of play for the one and two year olds in a nursery, there are some important basic *organisational points* which should be observed if there is to be maximum satisfaction for the children. These can be summarised in the following way.

- The types of objects provided should be of at least fifteen varieties, one bag for each kind. Bag size should be 16ins by 20ins with a cord to pull and close. Each bag is to be hung up when not in use. The amount of items should be ample, as already mentioned, that is, 50 to 60 curtain rings, pegs and so on. For a group of eight children, at least 20 receptacles are required, tins (with smooth edges), small baskets, and so on.

- For the period when the bags are used a clear space is needed, as large as possible, preferably carpeted. This makes for quietness which is an important feature of the session. It is better to put the other play material away during the period chosen for this activity.

- A limited period of the day should be selected and reserved for heuristic play. One hour, 10.00am to 11.00am has been found to be a good time. It is important to arrange a time when the

maximum of staff are present so that one member of staff can devote her full attention to a small group, (maximum of six to eight children). If during this period a child should need changing this is best done by another member of staff.

- The whole of the space available should be utilised to avoid the children crowding together. To this end the adult responsible should place the materials and the varied receptacles as far apart as possible. On the basis of her observation the adult will choose which of the types of material in each bag will make an interesting combination to offer to the children, for instance, chains, cylinders, curtain rings and pom-poms. Once the various materials are on the floor the children will choose what they want to experiment with without any direction or encouragement from the adult. Children need time to consider how they play with the material. The role of the adult is to give tranquil attention. When the children are concentrating, talking is superfluous.

- Naturally, all the objects which the children are exploring will soon be lying all over the floor and at some moments during the session the adult should do some unobtrusive reordering so that the material looks inviting all the time.

- The adult, keeping an eye on the clock, should allow sufficient time for unhurried clearing up, so that tidying away the items is as enjoyable as the activity of playing. It should be the children who actually collect the items from the floor, bringing them to the adults, popping them into the individual bags which they hold open for them. As each object is put in, the adult can check it to see that it is in good order, eliminating any ones which need replacing. In doing this they show by their attitude that they care for the material even if it consists of common household objects and 'junk'.

- As they supervise the collecting the adults can use simple comments, such as 'there's one under there', 'behind the chair', 'one by your foot'. In this way the child is practising selection and hearing phrases which are linked directly to an action. Note that when the adult decides that it is time to start clearing up it is important not to make a general appeal. If the adult calls 'Who is going to help me?', there is always the risk that this question may be answered with 'Not me!'. It is advised that the adult gives a nearby child, for example, a hair curler, and indicates by gesture that she should put it into the open proffered bag, and then look for the other curlers lying around, and then collect them, and so on with the other items. In this way the children are practising discrimination and selection until the whole floor is cleared, and there is a general feeling of having done the job together. It is here that the comments mentioned above come in useful.

THE ROLE OF THE ADULT

The role of the adult is partly that of organiser in collecting, caring for and thinking up new types of interesting items. They select different bags for use in each session, spacing them out on the available floor space for the children to choose from, and setting out the varied receptacles, baskets and tins. They unobtrusively reorder objects and initiate the collecting by the children, and the putting away of the materials in bags. They are essentially facilitators, and as such they remain quiet, attentive and observant. They may study a particular child and note down all that he or she does with the material, recording the quality of the child's concentration. The children are fully aware of their presence, though they do not encourage or suggest, praise or direct what the children do. (Only if a child begins to throw things about and disturb the others is it a wise plan to offer a receptacle and encourage her to place the things into it).

It is not suggested that a heuristic play session should be offered to the children every day and the staff should use their judgement about this. It is possible to be very flexible. A selection of the bags can easily be transported to any clear quiet space. One available adult can take a very small group and give them special attention. This can be particularly helpful to individual children who are unsettled, and who may find it difficult to enjoy playing.

Staff who have experienced conducting this kind of play session have noted that:

* an atmosphere of tranquil concentration develops;

* children become absorbed in pursuing their own exploration of the material for

periods of half an hour and more, without direct reference to the adult;

* conflicts between the children are very infrequent because there is abundant material, but at the same time there are many friendly interchanges between them, with gestures and early verbal comment;

* during the long nursery day this activity brings calm enjoyment both for them and for the adults. The staff have an opportunity to observe the children in a way which is not easy at other times in the busy day;

* where there are children under the age of two years in a mixed age group, it is possible, when there is a staff member available, for her to give some special attention to a very small group. It offers a great advantage since often the younger children find they have to compete for attention with the older ones;

* as soon as a child begins to have some command of language the nature of her use of the material changes and items are put to an imaginative use as another, more complex, type of play emerges. Instead of, 'What can I *do* with it?', the question moves to, 'What can this object become?'. For example, a wooden cylinder instead of being popped through a hole may be used as a feeding bottle for a doll. To link this to the Treasure Basket phase the same cylinder has been used, by the seated baby, to grasp, suck and bang with.

REFERENCES

Goldschmied, E. (1987) *Infants at Work* (Notes). Available from Early Childhood Unit, National Children's Bureau

Stroh, K. and Robinson, T. (1991) 'Developmental Delay in Young Children: Redressing the balance for child and parents'. *Child Language and Teaching Therapy 7, 1, 1-26.*

PATTERNS IN PAINTINGS, PATTERNS IN PLAY: YOUNG CHILDREN LEARNING

Nutbrown, C. (1989) 'Patterns in Paintings, Patterns in Play: Young Children Learning' *Topic: practical applications of research in education.* Spring. NFER-NELSON

Attempts to explain the intellectual development of young children are essentially cognitive theories, denoting stages of development and patterns of behaviour which children can be expected to demonstrate during their early years. While Piaget's (1926) studies of cognitive structure fill the gap in our understanding of children's development, there remains a lack of knowledge about how young children think about the world. Current theories concentrate on what children cannot do rather than consider and build on their achievements and capabilities.

From birth children possess patterns or 'schemas', such as sucking and grasping. As children grow, these schemas increase in number and complexity, and become coordinated with one another. Early schemas form the bases of the patterns of behaviour which children show between the ages of two and five.

Piaget used the notion of schema to illuminate the behaviour of babies under 18 months, but he did not continue this with children between two and five. However in her work at the Froebel Institute in London, Chris Athey has focused on how two- to five-year-olds also work on particular patterns of behaviour (Athey, 1981). She referred to each of these patterns as a 'schema' - 'a pattern of repeatable and generalisable actions which can be applied to objects or events'.

At the Institute she observed children, identified what schemas they took on and then nourished and extended them through a wide range of experiences. These included weekly visits to places and museums, providing materials for experiment and representation, and offering adult support and intervention. Such experiences were an attempt to fit the curriculum offered to the predominant schematic interests of each child. For example, a child exploring objects which rotated might have a predominant interest in rotation and circular objects. This can be called a 'dynamic circular' schema. The curriculum content to nourish this pattern of interest might include a visit to see a working water-wheel, watching tyres being changed on a vehicle, opportunities to look for and collect circular objects, and using a drill or vice on a workbench.

The early years practitioner will recognise in these experiences elements of mathematical and scientific learning which are essential in the curriculum. One aim of a curriculum based on schematic theory is to spot a child's schema and nourish it with worthwhile curriculum content. Matching what the teacher offers with what a child is doing and showing an interest in it can promote that child's motivation and development.

The children in Athey's Froebel project made highly significant gains in IQ and other standardised tests. These gains may be attributed to matching curriculum content to a child's schema, and to the involvement of parents who worked with their child and spotted the child's schema, then validated and extended its development with support and guidance from the project's professionals.

A child's schema can be seen as the core of the developing mind and thus a central element of intellectual growth. If it is so central to the child's thinking and doing, curriculum experiences are more likely to be absorbed if related to such a core.

IDENTIFYING SCHEMAS AND EXTENDING DEVELOPMENT

Awareness of children's patterns of learning and predominant interests contributed significantly to my own understanding of how children develop knowledge in the early years. To identify a schema, I observed children at work in the nursery setting over a period of time. I noted the choices they made, how they used materials and how they moved, and I collected and analysed their paintings.

I found certain patterns emerging. Children seemed to work on particular patterns of behaviour and movement which match those found in their early mark-making. For example, one child's pattern of behaviour indicated an interest in circular motion with the oval as a central mark in her paintings.

Athey identified a large number of schemas which many children portrayed during her Froebel project. My work drew on two of these schemas: the dynamic vertical and the enclosure schemas (Nutbrown, 1987).

1: THE DYNAMIC VERTICAL SCHEMA

In the nursery where I worked, I watched children playing with the range of materials available for them to explore. Alice (4 years 5 months) and James (3 years 11 months) were both absorbed by things that moved up and down. I watched Alice as she used the slide in the nursery garden. As she played, I described her actions to her: 'You're running up, spreading your arms, holding on to the bar. Now you're turning round and running down the slide again'.

Tait and Roberts (1974) consider that this technique of reflecting back a child's actions through language aids the development of talk and vocabulary. I used it here to develop language, validate the child's actions, help her to represent her own actions symbolically through language and extend the dynamic vertical schema.

Alice seemed to be absorbed with what I was saying but she continued her actions silently. Later that day, I watched her playing on the slide again and heard her say: 'Up the slide and down the slide.'

While James painted vertical marks on paper, I described his actions to him as I had with Alice: 'Those are interesting marks, James. You're making up and down marks.' James smiled and made other similar marks. When he had finished his painting, I invited James to talk about it. He said: 'That's Spiderman and he's jumping from the top to right down there'. As he spoke, he made a red mark from the top to the bottom of his page.

Alice demonstrated her vertical schema by:

- choosing equipment that enabled her to move up and down;

- moving up and down repeatedly;

- using the words 'up' and 'down'.

I nourished this pattern of interest by:

- making time, space and materials available for her to choose and use the equipment;

- observing her actions;

- matching my verbal input to her actions.

James demonstrated his vertical schema by:

- making vertical marks in paint;

- making a verbal description of his work which included the notion of 'going down'.

I nourished this pattern of interest by:

- making time, space and materials available for him to choose and use this activity;

- providing a verbal validation of his actions, using vocabulary which matched the marks he was painting;

- inviting James to discuss his mark-making.

Here these two simple examples illustrate how the adult can match her intervention with the child's schematic concern. Representing that schema in speech by adult or child is important, because the development of language is crucial in the early years, and speech used to symbolise activity is at a higher developmental level than that of silent activity.

2: THE ENCLOSURE SCHEMA

As Alice and James showed interest in vertical movements, other children in the nursery focused on putting things inside other things. Athey identifies notions of 'enclosure', 'containing', 'enveloping' and 'surrounding', which all appear to form a closely related cluster around an 'enclosure' schema.

Jeanette (4 years 3 months) worked on filling and emptying containers, developing her knowledge of weight, volume and the process of logical reasoning. She filled a jug with water and stood it upright. Then she tried to make an empty plastic bottle stand upright; when it wouldn't, Jeanette said: 'Oh! I know why it won't stand up .... because it's got no water in it.' She seemed to reason that the weight of water made the bottle stable.

Jeanette was making clear choices in the equipment she used and seemed to prefer activities which enabled her to get inside boxes, tunnels and houses, or to put things inside containers, shopping bags, buckets of sand and kitchen cupboards. Paper bags were provided in a 'play' shop to extend opportunities for filling and containing. Jeanette went into mass production of packages, filling bags with a variety of contents. Later she gave a bag to each adult in the nursery, saying 'It's for you'.

The forms of thought being exercised are 'containing', 'volume', 'capacity' and 'one-to-one correspondence'. After giving the staff their filled bags, Jeanette said proudly: 'I helped Ben to make this present for his mum. I showed him how.' Schematic behaviour is not purely cognitive; it also has an affective and social side.

RELATING SCHEMAS OF MOVEMENT AND SPEECH TO GRAPHIC SCHEMAS

Many teachers recognise the schematic threads which children in the early years weave through their mark-making. Paintings, drawings and early writing seem united in the patterns or schemas which pervade them. Teachers know which child has produced the 'patch'-painting and which has managed a tentative oval because they are aware of the current predominant interests in each child's mark-making. The marks children make can be a fruitful source of information on their current schematic concerns.

Such was the case with Jeanette. She dipped a model car into paint and made horizontal tracks which she connected to a wide arc. She placed dots inside the enclosure and named it 'Cars in a car park' (Figure 1). Both the graphic and speech representations reflected her interest in areas of space which enclose or surround objects.

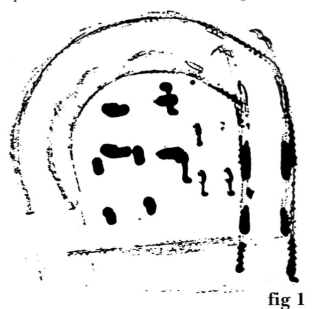

fig 1

Another drawing (Figure 2) showed two core and radial patterns each enclosed by a line. She added the ubiquitous dots, and described it as: 'It's the rain, and that's the umbrella. Those are the metal things and that's the material that covers over. And that's the spider. It's inside the sink, that's the sink.' Young children usually represent grid or core and radial spokes of an umbrella before they use the conventional, enclosed semicircle to represent the umbrella.

fig 2

Jeanette's drawings also indicated the cluster of elements connected with 'surrounding' and 'covering', and her descriptions of drawings of 'Snowman, snow all around' and 'A car covered in snow' further revealed the schematic influence. Often Jeanette put herself inside dens, boxes or brick enclosures. At one point, she sorted through the dressing-up clothes, then enclosed herself inside the trolley on which they were stored. She pretended the clothes were curtains and hung them all around the trolley. She kept saying 'Come in', implying she was inside some kind of dwelling. Later she got inside the climbing frame and said: 'This is my house; I'm in bed.'

IMPLICATIONS FOR EDUCATION IN THE EARLY YEARS

A great deal of learning can take place in early education around the simple but fundamental theme of what kinds of things can be found or put inside different containers, such as wrapping up cookery, animals that live in shells or holes, or caves and tunnels.

The curriculum is often presented to children through means of a theme or topic, which helps to provide them with a wide range of experience. The schematic theory endorses current thinking about providing broad areas of experience, facilitating and extending learning through play, and building on children's individual needs and experiences. It seems to link theory with practice, providing a closer link between the offered curriculum and what the child receives. This is possible because curriculum material can be planned as an extension of what the child has already shown an interest in through action, speech and graphic representations.

Children under five can be offered a wide array of experiences because they are likely to assimilate and enjoy such events. Extending themes of 'inside', 'surrounding' and 'outside' lends itself to linguistic, mathematical, scientific, musical, culinary and environmental areas of experience. Those three- and four-year-olds in the nursery seemed capable of exploring concepts at a higher level than current 'deficit' theory (focussing on what children cannot do) suggests is possible.

Schematic theory, which illuminates schematic behaviour, provides the key which opens the door to a wealth of learning. Closely watching the things children do, and identifying what they pay attention to, enables the teacher better to match curriculum content to a child's identified schemas.

Children's predominant schema seem to provide their motivation for learning - an insatiable drive to move, make representations in paint and to talk. They seem to make clear choices in their play, drawing from their environment the elements matching the schema that currently absorb them.

Schemas seem to make children alert to certain events and properties of objects in their environment. When professionals learn to identify these concerns, they are better placed to select appropriate curricular provision because their practice can be more clearly informed by and related to theory.

Some of the more powerful schemas are those concerned with the movement of objects - things that go up and down, back and forth or in a circular direction. Athey showed that each of such schemas goes through different stages from early motor level to symbolic representation.

In my own study the curriculum presupposed the value of learning through play, and started from a child's individual needs and interests, nurturing the child's chosen content and action.

All this helped to ensure that schemas were met with a wealth of worthwhile curriculum content offered by adults and accompanied by much adult intervention. A wide range of 'open-ended' equipment was provided, backed by the notion of 'a place for everything and everything in its place'.

Planning and organising the curriculum must take account of the need to nourish schematic concerns of individual children, and to provide a wide-ranging curriculum fostering broad areas of experience. Staff might plan provision in terms of the tools for the task, but the children decide on the nature of the work. For example, equipment for sand, water and clay can be provided in accessible containers. A child choosing to play with water can select from the range of equipment which might be used to extend a number of schemas. The equipment chosen and how it is used suggests which schema a child is working on.

A child working on dynamic vertical schema might choose to experiment with dropping various objects and materials from a height into the water. A child interested in containing or enclosing might fill containers with clay, sand or water. The first child can learn about gravity, flotation and immersion, while the second can explore the concepts of capacity, size and volume. Both children, working at their own level of development, find out about the properties of water. Adult intervention can be matched to each child's activity, as appropriate. Such developments can help teachers in early education because interpreting children's behaviour at this schematic level can lead to a more effective early years curriculum, building upon and extending current practices.

The views expressed in this article are personal and do not necessarily reflect the policies of the local authority for which I work.

NOTES

Cathy Nutbrown is Under Fives Coordinator at Sheffield Education Department.
Address for correspondence: 9 Oakworth Drive, Halfway, Sheffield S19 5SB.

The information reported in 'Patterns in paintings, patterns in play: young children learning' represents a small part of a wider study undertaken as a dissertation written at Sheffield City Polytechnic.

Current work continues to look at schemas and explores curriculum development possibilities with older children. The author is also working with a group of teachers considering links between schemas and writing throughout the 3-12 age range.

Information reported upon resulted from experiences gained while working as a teacher researcher, and following a degree course part-time.

REFERENCES

Athey, C. (1981) 'Parental involvement in nursery education', *Early Child Development and Care,* 7, 4.

Piaget, J. (1926) *The Language and Thought of the Child.* London: Routledge and Kegan Paul.

Nutbrown, C.E. (1987) *'A case study of the development and implementation of a nursery curriculum based on schematic theory'.* Unpublished dissertation, Sheffield City Polytechnic.

Tait, M. and Roberts, M. (1974) *Play, Language and Experience.* Organisation Mondiale pour l'Education Prescolaire.

Copying Permitted: The NFER-NELSON Publishing Company grants to education institutions and interested bodies permission to reproduce this item in the interests of wider dissemination.

ANOTHER WAY OF LOOKING

Armstrong, M. (1990) 'Another Way of Looking'
Forum. 33, 1, 12-16.

Two years ago, at Forum's last London conference, I argued that the National Curriculum amounted to a betrayal of children. That, of course, was before we knew the details, when all was mere outline. Two years on, many details are still obscure, but enough is clear to permit a fuller judgement. That judgement must still be that the National Curriculum betrays the children whose intellectual interests it is supposed to serve.

I say this despite the well-intentioned efforts of liberal teachers to play the National Curriculum game in the hope of subverting its rules. It seems to me that any attempt to gentle the National Curriculum is necessarily futile because that curriculum is framed in terms which miscontrue the nature of learning and of teaching. The narrow specification of the curriculum by subject ignores the way in which the course of learning proceeds in imaginative classrooms. The language of targets and levels of attainment reduces achievement to a false hierarchy of technical accomplishments. The unacknowledged metaphor of 'delivery' deprives children of their constructive and reconstructive role in the acquisition of knowledge.

For me, the moment of truth had a very particular location - paragraph 10.19 of the first report of the National Curriculum English Working Group, **English for ages 5 to 11**. This first report is the most progressive to have emerged so far. Over and over again the report insists on the importance of attending to the significance of what children have to say rather than to its apparent form. Teachers are urged to show 'respect for and interest in the learner's language, culture, thought and intentions'. It is suggested that teachers provide the greatest encouragement for children to communicate in writing when they respond more to the content of what is written than to errors of letter formation, spelling and composition. 'Meaning' we are told, 'should always be in the foreground'.

Until, that is, we reach paragraph 10.19. For there we read: 'The best writing is vigorous, committed, honest and interesting. We have not included these qualities in our attainment targets because they cannot be mapped onto levels. Even so, all good classroom practice will be geared to encouraging and fostering these vital qualities'.

That last sentence reads as a desperate attempt to avoid the implication of what has just been said. For this paragraph can only mean that meaning itself, its quality, its value, is not to be assessed within the National Curriculum and finds no legitimate place among its 'clear objectives'. Look through the attainment targets carefully. You will find among the Working Group's slender description not a single trace of meaning. It is true that Attainment Target No3 is defined as 'a growing ability to construct and convey meaning in written language'. But nowhere does the character or quality of a child's meanings feature among the statements of attainment, level on level, that follow this opening definition. Meaning is central but meaning is not to be assessed. Children may be 'makers of meanings in their own texts' but the meanings they make are unexaminable.

It says a good deal for the honesty of the English Working Group that it has so frankly acknowledged the irrelevance of meaning to the language of attainment targets, the language that has determined the National Curriculum. In this, as in much else, it has the advantage over the National Curriculum Council. Indeed it is worth pausing a moment to notice the National Curriculum Council's way with paragraph 10.19. Acknowledging the alarm of many teachers at the implications of the paragraph, the Council claims to have 'undertaken the task of mapping such qualities (as vigour, independence and commitment) on to levels in its recommended statements of attainment'. This specious claim is a choice example of the Council's piecemeal and extempore methods.

It was not until the publication of the English Working Group's *second* report - (by which time paragraph 10.19 had become paragraph

17.31) that the National Curriculum Council took any notice of the notorious paragraph. By that time Levels 1 to 3 of the Attainment Targets for English had already been determined by statutory order, following the recommendations of the Council itself. They could not be revised again. So Levels 1 to 3 still contain no reference to qualities of meaning. It is charitable to attribute this to the Council's oversight. Or is it that the Council considers children below Level 4 to be incapable of significant utterance?

In the end it hardly matters, for when at Level 4 the National Curriculum Council at last proceeds to revise the Working Group's statements of attainment to take account of meaning it does so in a manner that is entirely frivolous. The Working Group had described Level 4 as the level at which children are able to 'Write stories which have an opening, a setting, characters, a series of events and a resolution'. To this admittedly banal definition of an average eleven year old's literary artistry the Council adds the words 'and which engage the sympathy and interest of the reader'. Just that - no more. Now it's important, who can doubt it, to engage a reader's interest, especially if that reader happens to be your teacher. But to suppose that this is enough to dispense with the problem of paragraph 10.19 - that reader response is the unique key to meaning - is at best careless.

There is no evidence in either of the National Curriculum Council's Consultation Documents on English in the National Curriculum to suggest that the Council has in any way understood the dilemma recognised by the Working Group. This is scarcely surprising. For what 10.19 shows us is that the language of the National Curriculum is impervious to the significance of children's thought and affords no access to an understanding of children's understanding, either of how to describe it or of how to promote it.

So what are we to do? How is it possible to rewrite the National Curriculum in language that restores meaning to its place at the centre of learning and teaching? I don't know the answer to this question but I think I know how to begin to find out. I would begin with interpretation. What does it mean to ascribe significance to children's thought and action, and to see that significance as the clue to learning and to teaching - the clue also to content and method in the curriculum? I want to approach this question through one particular instance. The English Working Group has once again provided the opportunity.

Appendix 6 of **English for ages 5 to 11** presents a series of illustrative examples of 'children's developing writing with reference to our attainment targets' as the Report puts it. Here is the fourth example, 'an unaided first draft by a middle infant girl'. (See page 3.32).

Here is how the English Working Group describes this wonderful tale, which is said to 'illustrate several Level 2 features of writing':

'This is a simple chronological account with a clear story structure, including a conventional beginning, narrative middle and end. The sentences are almost all demarcated, though via the graphic, comic-strip layout and not via capital letters and punctuation. The spelling is almost entirely meaningful and recognisable. In several cases, it shows that the author has correctly grasped the patterns involved, even though the individual spellings are wrong (eg trooth, eny, owt, sumthing, cubad). The handwriting occasionally mixes upper and lower case letters, though only at beginnings and ends of words, not at random'.

That is all the Working Group has to say about 'When I was naughty'. It's all that the National Curriculum requires it to say. Is that really all a six year old writer can do? Is that all her knowledge, skill and understanding amount to? Is that all that's worth saying about this story? Is it, at any rate, all we need to record, all we need to know, as parents, teachers, storytellers ourselves? Can this really be how to talk about children and their work? For myself, I can't imagine a thinner description of a young child's narrative achievement. At no point is there the smallest recognition of the story's significance, of the relationship between its meaning and its form, of the quality of narrative thought which is seeking expression here. Any teacher who attempted no more than this would have little chance of understanding this child's understanding, let alone of promoting it. If this is really how we are expected to evaluate our pupils, we're surely in the wrong trade.

So let's take a close look at the story.

'When I was naughty' examines the moral order and its relation to experience, as seen from the perspective of six years old. It deals with questions of truth and lying, mutuality and recrimination, guilt and blame. It addresses, at least implicitly, the conflict between a child's and an adult's view of these matters. One of the most striking aspects of the story is the way the narrative dramatises the interlocking conflicts which make up its subject matter. And the drawings play as important part in this drama as the writing.

'It was a few weeks past my birthday when me and my sister went to the kitchen.' There's a feeling of a formula about this opening, and yet, compared with 'Once upon a time' it's strikingly precise. It marks out what is to come as a reminiscence - fact - rather than a fairy tale. Might it be more than a formula though? 'A few weeks past my birthday ....'. Might that birthday signify the coming of a new age, the age of moral awareness, a new maturity? Part of the business of interpretation is to persuade ourselves that such speculations are appropriate, even to a six year old's story.

The second frame is all uninhibited action. 'I went to the cupboard and Clare opened the cupboard and we took the crisps and we went upstairs'. The tiny, canonical sentences hurry by, each with its active verb in a simple past tense - 'went', 'opened', 'took', 'went', - each linked to the next by an indispensable 'and'. How beautifully the first three drawings express the impulse of this action. In the first drawing one child is already in the kitchen, approaching the cupboard, while the other crosses the living room with its large round central light. By the second drawing both children have reached the kitchen and Clare is already at the cupboard, stretching up to remove the crisps. The living room is empty. What a way for a six year old to picture movement! The third drawing, which really belongs with the second frame, shows the two children striding upstairs, the leading one in the act of stepping from one stair to the other, caught in the act, as she is just about to be.

So far in the story there's been no trace of the moral order, unless we choose to read the words 'the cupboard' as suggestive of a guarded space, or the words 'the crisps' as hinting at the fatefulness of the object taken. The two children seem to be acting without constraint. Nothing yet has been forbidden them. It's fascinating to see how subtly the storyteller emphasises the mutuality of the sisters at this point in their adventures. '*Me and my sister* went' .... '*I* went' .... '*Clare* opened' .... ' *We* took' .... '*We* went upstairs'. And now a sudden eruption: dad, lies, punishment, recrimination, the world of moral order.

The author is remarkably particular about this shift. At the end of frame two the flow of action is brought sharply to a stop. Could it be

significant that the break comes with the last word of frame two rather than with the first word of frame three? Every other frame closes on a full stop. Not this one though. Is the writer trying to highlight the interruption of the action in full flow? In a complementary move the drawing that follows in frame three is still bound up with the interrupted action, as if the momentum of the previous frame has overflown, so to speak, its own arrest.

'My dad caught me and Clare ....' 'Caught': this one word transforms everything that has gone before, turning the children's freedom of action into a transgression, a flouting of the rules. 'Caught', not 'met' or 'saw' or 'came across'. At once the guilty deed is exposed. 'So he said'. That 'so' is significant too. The OED tells us that the particle 'so' denotes both sequence and consequence, sometimes both at once.

So it is here. The 'so' of the story - and I think it could be argued that the lack of punctuation here is an advantage, heightening the double significance of 'so' - implies, surely, that dad has already guessed the truth. From here on all that will count is the acknowledgement of what is already recognised as guilt.

See how the drawing to frame four captures the moment of truth. Dad has appeared in a doorway at the foot of the stairs on which the two sisters are suddenly frozen. The leading sister's striding foot has dropped back a step. It's a beautifully observed detail.

I love the confessional scene, the way it escalates. 'So, he said have you took something from the cupboard? No. we said. Then my dad said, have you? No, I lied. Are you telling lies? No, no, no, I lied again.' The rhetoric of this passage is wonderfully artful. It has all the storyteller's flair. But the artfulness is surely born of a certain familarity, and with more than the single event which the story tells, assuming it's a true story. Observation, memory and art are almost inseparable here, though I suppose we might wonder about that 'have you took'.

This is the moment at which the mutuality of the sisters begins to break down. It is the narrator alone, in the end, who is made to tell the truth. 'No *we* said .... no *I* lied .... no no no *I* lied again ... in the end my dad made *me* tell the truth.' Divide and rule; it's as if our six year old storyteller has seen it all.

'In the end my dad made me tell the truth.'

When I was naughty

It was a ferw weex Past my birthday wen me and my sister went to the Kitchen

I went to the Cubad and Clare opnd the cubad and We tuck the crips and We went up seris My

dad cort me and Clare so he said have you Tuck Sum thing From the cubad no we said

then My dad Said have you noIlid are you teling lis no no no I lid again In the end My dad Mad me tell the trooth

then he said you naughty gils and Sent me and Clare to bed With owt eny Supa And Clare blamd it on Me.

Young writers sometimes have an enviable knack of cutting a long story short. We do not need to know the how of it. The point is that it's impossible to get away with it. A father's authority is sufficient to get at the truth. Or perhaps it's his trickiness, his deviousness. I think it's worth observing that the storyteller offers no comment, either as to the rightness or wrongness of the father's forcing the truth or indeed of the sisters' taking of the crisps in the first place. We may interpret the morality as we will. We are presented only with the outcome. It's characteristic of young children's stories to be open in this way.

Finally, then, retribution. 'Then he said, you naughty girls, and sent me and Clare to bed without any supper and Clare blamed it on me.' In frame two the sisters appeared to be in control of their own destiny - 'we took the crisps and we went upstairs'. Now the tables are turned. Instead of went we find 'sent' - 'sent to bed without any supper'. The girls after all are subject to their father's will. In the final drawing the stairs have grown steeper, almost mountainous. They are no longer the quick, easy passage from kitchen cupboard to children's room. Now they mark the sad, slow ascent to the place of punishment. Clare has disappeared, appropriately enough since the father's intervention has destroyed the sisters' mutuality. 'And Clare blamed it on me'. The narrator, who in acknowledging her guilt gave the game away, is left to face her father's anger alone as he stands at the foot of the stairs, enforcing his order.

So what are we to make of one tiny story, however charming?

The English Working Group chose it to illustrate the meagre account of attainment set out in their statutory targets and levels. It is more appropriately read, first as an indictment of that account, and second as a clue to an alternative account. For there is another way of looking.

'When I was naughty' allows us to glimpse a young child's thought in all its imaginative richness. The artistry of its six year old author is apparent in every aspect of her story. In her exploitation of narrative style, with its formulas, its suspense, its various concealments and revelations, its openness to interpretation. In her acceptance of constraint and her turning of constraint into opportunity; think of her virtuoso treatment of the limited sentence structure available to her at this point in her

narrative development, the way she makes use of the conjunction 'and' and the particle 'so'. In her critical judgement, so apparent in her choice of vocabulary. In her concern to express her own sense of life in the ordered medium of written and drawn narrative. In short, in her appropriation of form.

For me the history of learning is the history of the appropriation of form, in this way and in countless other ways, while the history of teaching begins and ends in the *interpretation* of appropriated form. By interpretation I mean the critical scrutiny of children's intellectual enterprise, from moment to moment and from subject matter to subject matter, over the course of children's school careers. The description which I've just attempted of 'when I was naughty' is an example of interpretation, as applied to one particular product of one particular child's intellectual enterprise at one particular moment in time. Multiplied across the curriculum and sustained over the years, a set of descriptions of this kind, accompanied by their objects - the works described and the evidence of the manner of their composition - would amount to an intellectual biography, a kind of documentary history of individual, and therefore incommensurate, achievement. This is what I mean by another way of looking and it is equally another way of speaking, as distant from the language of attainment targets as it is possible to imagine.

The focus of interpretation is a child's thought and action at its most significant. Our interest, in interpretation, is not in simulations of thought - exercises, tests, prescribed tasks, standard procedures - but in the work which is most expressive of each child's struggle with meaning. As far as the study of English is concerned, that includes children's stories and poems, diaries and notebooks, arguments and conversations, play acting and make believe, reflections and speculations on language and literature.

One of the most important tasks in interpreting children's work is to describe its patterns of intention: the interests, motifs, orientations, forms of meditation that govern a child's thought and seek expression in her practice. The concerns expressed in a story like 'When I was naughty' are clear enough, some of them at any rate: concerns, for example, with family relationships, with issues of loyalty, deceit and authority, concerns which further examples of the author's work would help us to evaluate more precisely.

A second task is to examine the interplay between form and content in a child's thought, and between technique and expression. The relationship of word to picture in 'When I was naughty' is an example of this kind of interplay, as is the author's manipulation of a limited range of sentence types to maximum effect.

A third task for interpretation is to trace the circulation of a child's ideas through all the various aspects of the curriculum. See how literature, art, moral thought, personal and social education are all implicated in our six year old's one story.

A single text has served me as an example of how to interpret children's thought; but this is in a way misleading, for it's characteristic of interpretation to be concerned with the development of a child's ideas from work to work over time - a week, month, year, career.

This is the moment at which it becomes necessary to talk about intervention as the natural complement of interpretation. Interpretation and intervention are the two faces of teaching, assuming that teaching is seen as a way of sustaining children's critical engagement with thought in all its forms. To interpret a six year old's story is to begin to understand her own understanding, and that in turn is to begin to understand how to promote further understanding. Interpretation sets the agenda for intervention. It suggests to us, in the case of 'When I was naughty', the stories the writer might read to aid her own writing or to develop her sense of literature. It shows us how to help her to address the moral concerns which dominate her narrative. It clarifies for us the interplay of words and pictures in the thought. It helps us to see how we might raise with her, however tentatively, the questions of narrative voice and narrative identity. It illustrates the significance which at this point in her development she attaches to punctuation; we notice the simple large full stop decisively placed at the end of her tale and wonder, maybe, how significant the matter of punctuation might seem to her just now.

It would be nice to imagine that the division of the National Curriculum's statutory orders into attainment targets and programmes of study reflected this distinction between interpretation and intervention. Nice but fanciful. The attainment targets have nothing to do with interpretation and for this reason they afford no purchase on intervention. It is the fatal weakness of the entire enterprise.

Many of the Working Groups, it is true, have sought to use the programmes of study to emphasise the wealth of learning and teaching that resists the language of targeting, and none more so than the English Working Group. Its two reports are quite adventurous about intervention. They describe the 'diverse role teachers will have to play in the development of young writers: they will be observers, facilitators, modellers, readers and supporters'. They insist that the 'teacher's response to written work should aim to foster a child's confidence in the exploration of ideas'. They ask teachers to write alongside their pupils in the classroom. They demand well-equipped classrooms full of books, notepads, post boxes, word-processors, play-houses. They suggest that 'opportunities should be provided .... to read and write lists, labels, letters, invitations, leaflets, pamphlets, plans and diagrams' not to mention 'diaries, stories and accounts of things'. They tell us to encourage children 'to share their writing with others, to discuss what they have written and to publish stories, newspapers, magazines, games and guides'.

Useful as these various statements are, they remain incoherent because of the failure to relate them to the interpretive outlook in which they gain their educational justification. It is not possible, for example, to make sense of the demand that teachers write alongside their pupils unless education is perceived as a common and collaborative struggle for meaning in which both teachers and taught have much to share and much to learn from each other, whether the pupils be five, or fifteen, or fifty years old.

In as much as it depends on the recognition and promotion of significant utterance, education thrives on conversation. Unfortunately conversation is at odds with the ideology that has inspired the National Curriculum. Laid down from above, expressed in the language of law, obsessed with standardisation, committed to a hierarchical model of achievement, the National Curriculum can only get in the way of the conversation that thrives in resourceful classrooms and sustains the course and the cause of learning. To rewrite that curriculum in a way which supports conversation will take a long time, and great political determination. I have suggested that a promising way to begin is to look at how we interpret children's thought. There are plenty of other ways too. Let the exploration begin.

MATCHING THE TASK TO THE PUPIL

F Alexander, R., Rose, J. and Woodhead, C. (1992)
Curriculum organisation and classroom practice in primary schools: a discussion paper
paras 107-116 Department of Education and Science

107   Standards of education in primary schools will not rise until teachers expect more of their pupils, and, in particular, more of able and disadvantaged children.

108   The problem is partly ideological. In some schools and local education authorities the legitimate drive to create equal opportunities for all pupils has resulted in an obsessive fear of anything which, in the jargon, might be deemed 'elitist'. As a consequence, the needs of some of our most able children have quite simply not been met. There has also been a tendency to stereotype, and, in particular, to assume that social disadvantage leads inevitably to educational failure. This waste of potential must not continue.

109   A second explanation lies in the classroom itself where a number of factors have combined to create a situation in which pupils may be set tasks which fail to challenge their level of understanding. The problem may be that the teacher's knowledge of the subject is inadequate. It may stem from a view of 'match', which, in emphasising a child's 'readiness' and requiring teachers to operate within some theoretical notion of what children of a given age or stage are capable of, positively invites low expectations. But research has shown that over-complex patterns of classroom organisation can also contribute to the problem. If teachers are submerged by low-level routine activities, they do not have the time needed for proper diagnosis and task matching. A reduction in class sizes and the use of non-teaching assistants would obviously remove some of the pressure, but teachers can and should, in our view, review how they currently organise their classrooms in order to ensure that they are making the most efficient use possible of one of the most valuable resources schools possess: teaching time.

110   Given that significant progress could be made through a more efficient use of teaching time, we must add that the idea that at any one time learning tasks in nine subjects can be exactly matched to the needs and abilities of all the pupils in a class is hopelessly unrealistic. Match and differentiation are critical to effective learning, but they are aspirations rather than absolutes. In current circumstances, the best the teacher can do (and it is a great deal) is to devise the classroom settings and pupil tasks which give the best chance of success.

ASSESSING AND RECORDING PROGRESS

111   HMI surveys since the 70s show that pupil assessment has often been a largely intuitive process. Records have been similarly idiosyncratic and have tended to be limited to the basics and to focus on tasks encountered rather than learning achieved. Until recently, parents often received generalised, laconic statements which offered little real insight into the progress their children had made.

112   Many schools and LEAs had attempted to address these problems before the introduction of the National Curriculum. There is no doubt, however, that, whatever the difficulties experienced in managing the first round of standard assessment tasks, National Curriculum assessment procedures have accelerated the development process. Assessment is now becoming more open, systematic and comprehensive.

113   It is clear from evidence gathered since the introduction of the National Curriculum that effective assessment and record keeping are more likely to occur in schools which recognise that pupils' progress depends upon assessing their strengths and weaknesses, and that records are needed to ensure the transmission of information from one teacher to another, from school to home and from school to school.

114   Classroom management and organisation are particularly critical to the quality of assessment. Teachers need to observe pupils systematically, to structure their

learning, and to monitor their progress. If they are to do this, then the classroom must be organised in a way which makes best use of the time they can devote to such activities. Classrooms where too many activities are going on at once risk forcing the teacher into time-wasting crisis management, rather than purposeful assessment.

115 One obvious aspect of assessment which needs emphasis is that pupils need genuine feedback about the success or otherwise of their learning. The evidence suggests that while pupils are generally clear about what they have to do, they often do not receive enough information about the purposes of their learning and, what is even more important, how well they are doing. Marking pupils' work is one valuable means of feedback, provided that it offers specific, diagnostic comment and not only encouragement. Although it is logistically difficult, the act of marking work in the pupil's presence is an even more effective approach. Pupils should as far as is feasible be involved in the assessment of their own work.

116 Assessment and record-keeping are not synonymous, though they are frequently treated as such. There is little point in developing an elaborate record-keeping system if the evidence upon which the records are based is inadequate. The pre-condition for good records is, therefore, good assessment. Indeed, there is some evidence that record keeping may become an end in itself: cumbersome, time consuming and of little value to either teacher or pupil. The purposes and recipients of records need to be clearly identified and the records constructed accordingly.

Making
Assessment
Work

ACTIVITY 3D   Can We Agree?

PREPARATION

Notes on flipcharts made during Activities 3B: **Stocktaking** and 3C: **Learning about learning.**

Notes to Group Leaders

In this activity colleagues who work together will consolidate their knowledge about children's learning and reach a statement of consensus to underpin their future work (keep the statement for Section Five). If there are people with very different views working together this could be a difficult process. Group members may need support in finding ways of acknowledging the views of others without leaving hold of their own strongly held beliefs.

INTRODUCTION TO THE ACTIVITY

During your work on this section, you have looked at patterns and pathways in your own learning. You have revisited your own learning about learning in the past, and you have thought about some recent descriptions of children's learning. Now you will consolidate and summarise all this thinking, so that you can work with your colleagues towards an agreed statement of what you all understand about children's learning.

The purpose of this activity is for you to:

*   make a collaborative statement about children's learning

LOOKING AT LEARNING

1. Working on your own, look back over all the work you have done on this section, especially in the last two activities. Try to summarise the most important elements of what you know about children's learning in a sentence or two - concisely enough to fit on a postcard! Make sure you include the word **learning.**

2. Work with colleagues from your own staff group to discuss what you have all written. Using each person's contributions, try to negotiate a common statement that you can all accept. Work hard to defend the ideas you feel are important, but be prepared to let go of minor oddities that other people in your staff group aren't prepared to work with.

3. Write your final statement up boldly on a large sheet of paper so that everyone can see what each small group has been doing. You will be able to look back at this statement and use it to support your work on finding the principles that underlie effective assessment (Section Five), and your work on finding an appropriate format for recording children's learning (Section Seven).

Making Assessment Work

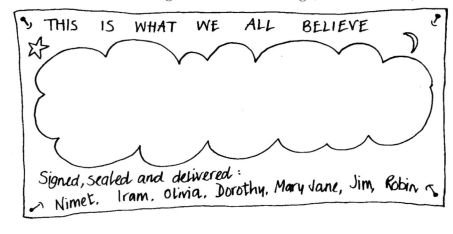

SECTION THREE: LOOKING AT LEARNING

The main themes of this section have been:

effective assessment is based on our growing understanding of how young children develop and learn

'in our view, each institution should have ...

an **approach to learning** geared to the needs of young children, which emphasises first hand experiences and which views **play** and **talk** as powerful mediums of learning; and which incorporates periods of time for sustained activity.'
Starting with Quality, DES 1990

REFERENCES

See selection in **Learning about learning.**

Bee, H. (1985) (fourth edition) *The Developing Child.* Harper and Row. Part Three - 'The Thinking Child'.

Benedict, R. (1946) *The Chrysanthemum and the Sword.* Charles E Tuttle Company. Vermont USA Chapter 12 - 'The Child Learns'.

Clark-Stewart, A. and Koch, J. (1983) *Children. Development through Adolescence.* John Wiley and Sons
Chapter 5 'Cognitive Development in Infancy'.
Chapter 6 'Cognitive Development in Early Childhood'.
Chapter 7 'Learning Language in Early Childhood'.

Drummond M.J. (1993) *Assessing Children's Learning.* David Fulton Press.

SECTION 4
Observations

4

INTRODUCTION

All educators of young children watch and listen to what children do and say. They watch to keep them safe, to find ways of pleasing them, to set limits on their behaviour, to understand and enjoy their activities, to find ways of extending their play and for hundreds of other reasons.

Watching and listening take many forms:

* watching for cues from a seven week old baby as she coos and babbles

* listening to a five-year-old's suggestion about what kind of glue to use as she works intently on her cardboard model

* listening for the feelings of a three-year-old patient in the home corner hospital

* watching and interpreting the eye movements and the pupil expansion of a child with cerebral palsy clamouring for another turn with the classroom rabbit on her lap.

Watching and listening like this can help adults to build relationships with children, and to interact sensitively with them.

Watching and listening in this way can also be the start of something rather different; in this section of the pack you will be able to think about the way in which watching and listening lead into the activity of **observing** children.

When educators observe children, at home, in family group settings, or in nursery, playgroup or classroom, they are doing something of immense importance in their work. In observing children, educators can move beyond what they see and hear and touch, and begin to make meaning of what they see, interpreting children's activities in the light of their experience. By setting time aside in the daily routine to make and use observations, educators are not indulging themselves, or opting out from interacting with children. They are making time for a professional necessity, focusing their experienced eyes on the children they educate and care for. This focused attention opens the doors to discovery and new understanding, to the possibility of fuller and more secure relationships, to a more complete knowledge of each child's growth and development.

In the busy daily routine, educators are sometimes under pressure: pressure to be efficient, to deliver the agreed programme, to tick the tick-sheets and check the check-lists, to be precisely accountable for everything they do. But observing children means more than this. By observing children, educators become accountable in a richer and more fulfilling way. They can account for children's emotional growth, their fantasies, their creativity and their play. They can give detailed descriptions of the challenges children meet, of their struggles to understand and master the world around them. They can give an account of every aspect of children's learning. Observing children plays a crucial part in developing and maintaining a quality curriculum for all children.

*Making
Assessment
Work*

In this section of the pack you will be able to explore a number of questions about the purposes and value of observations in your work with young children. You will be able to ask yourselves:

- what are the most important purposes for observing young children?

- do you need special techniques for observing, or just your eyes and ears?

- how can you use your experience of working with children over the years to enrich your observations, making them more meaningful, to yourself and others?

- how can you become more confident in interpreting what you see and hear, trying to understand children's thinking and learning?

- how do you decide on the practicalities of observation - how, who, what, where and when?

- how can observation make your work with children more rewarding?

The purposes of this section are for you to:

- think about some (or all) of these questions

- review the observation methods you already use

- experiment with some techniques that may be new to you, and decide if they would be useful in your work

- explore the ways in which observation can be part of your daily routines, helping you to support young children's learning and development

- think about ways of involving parents in the process of observation, at home and in the work place

There are five activities in this section; the first is an opportunity to review present practice, and is followed by three activities focusing on improving practice. You will be able to decide for yourselves, depending on the experience of your group, how much time you want to give to these activities, or a selection from them. The fifth activity is both reflective and developmental, supporting you in applying what you have learned from your work on this section.

*Making
Assessment
Work*

ACTIVITY 4A	What do we do now?

PREPARATION

Flip chart sheets
Pens and notebooks
Copies of the Handout

from 30 minutes
to 1 hour 30
minutes
depending on the
experience of the
group members

Notes to Group Leaders

It is difficult to predict the amount of time needed for this activity. It will depend on the experience of the group members, and the variety of their present practices. Some of them may already systematically use different types of observation in their work, while others may be new to the idea of any kind of regular planned observation. There may be very different understandings of the purpose and value of observation, and you will need to allow time to explore this issue fully and sensitively.

INTRODUCTION TO THE ACTIVITY

The purposes of this activity are for you to:

• list all the ways in which you observe children, by watching, listening and making notes

• think about the purpose and value of observation for you, in your workplace

1. Working as a whole group, make a long list (on a flip chart sheet) of all the ways in which you could be said to observe the children you work with, however informal or spontaneous these ways may seem.

2. Read Handout 4A, which gives some personal definitions of observation written by early years educators who worked with the trial version of this pack. Which of these definitions best describes the things that you and your colleagues do? Discuss your different views in the whole group.

   If none of these descriptions seems to fit what you do, spend a few minutes writing a definition of your own observation practices, and sharing it with the whole group.

3. Working in a small group of two or three, look over the whole list of what people do, and talk about which of these ways of observing children seem to have most value for you, in your work place.

4. To round off the activity, work as a whole group to talk about what observation means to you. Imagine that a 15-year-old has come to your workplace for work experience, because s/he is thinking about working with young children. How would you explain that observation is part of your job?

HANDOUT 4A   Definitions

1. 'Observation means being aware of what children are doing - all the time picking up instances which tell you something about the child.'
    day nursery principal

2. 'Observation: actually watching children. It needn't be like a time set apart, where you just sit at the back. It can be a part of every activity.'
    student teacher

3. 'Observing is becoming part of the scene, becoming attuned to children's thoughts and feelings through watching their play. But by watching we become a part, as soon as we look it changes.'
    social worker - group day care

4. 'Observing playgroup children gives playgroup leaders more confidence in their ability to run a high quality care group, because they know exactly what's going on.'
    preschool playgroup tutor

5. 'To be useful observation needs to be a kind of "snapshot" of the child - something which gives a good idea of how he or she is developing.'
    nursery teacher

6. 'Observations are a way of taking time out to study and record a young child's development.'
    student nursery nurse

7. 'Having eyes in the back of your head!'
    childminder - family day care

8. 'The knowledge you gain from observing children helps you understand and respect them.'
    playgroup leader

9. 'Observation means watching my children's play at home, and noting down anything interesting in the home-school diary.'
    parent

10. 'Absorbing the moments of learning when you see children grasp a concept - writing it down quickly! '
    nursery teacher

one hour

| ACTIVITY 4B | Getting started |

PREPARATION

Pens and notebooks
Copies of the two Handouts
Flipchart or sheets of large paper

Notes to Group Leaders

Some members of the group may not have had much experience of deliberately setting aside time for carefully planned observations, while, for others, structured observations may already be part of their established routine. Some group members may need a good deal of support in considering ways of working that may seem difficult and unfamiliar at first.

INTRODUCTION TO THE ACTIVITY

In this activity you will discuss some of the different purposes of making observations of young children, so that you can ensure that the observations you make, in your workplace, will be meaningful, manageable, and worthwhile. You will think about some of the different things educators do as part of their work:

interacting with children	or	observing from a distance
being busy	or	keeping quiet and still
doing things for children	or	watching them do things on their own

The purposes of the activity are for you to:

- look at some practical stages in making observations

- think about the implications for other people of using observations in your workplace

- think about the underlying reasons for making and using observations in particular ways

1. Working in small groups, look at the Handout provided **I want to know .....** Are these the kinds of things you might 'want to know' in your work place, about the children you work with? Jot down some extra examples of your own.

2. Now work with the same group to think about how you would set about finding out what you 'want to know'. The Handout **Starting points** shows some of the practical decisions you will have to make. You will want to add some more details of your own in the empty boxes provided.

   Select one aspect of a child's (or children's) learning and development that you 'want to know' about, and, using the Handout, make a list of the preparations and decisions you need to make. Be sure to check on the reasons behind each decision - using the WHY in each box as a reminder of the need to justify what you decide to do.

3. Working as a whole group, identify:

   - a selection of the ideas and decisions that have been stimulated by the **Starting points** Handout

   - the most contentious issue you discussed

I want to know how the children are using the new set of Chinese bowls and chopsticks in the home area. I want to observe children playing on their own, and the interaction between the children and the adults, so that we can assess if we are implementing our policy of challenging racism in the nursery, and whether it's having any effect.

I am worried about Samuel's hearing. I want to find out if he can hear the stories, instructions and conversations with his key worker. I want to know if Sam's mother and father share my concern.

I want to know if children are having enough time with play of their own choice to allow for sustained, self-initiated activity and problem-solving during the daily routine. I want to know if the parent helpers have noticed anything important about the children's choices.

I want to know whether Shafiq is using both English and Urdu during the day. Mrs S is worried that he doesn't seem to want to speak Urdu at home any more; I must check out that the other educators are aware of Shafiq's ability to speak two languages, before I make another appointment with her.

It is our policy to encourage men to participate in the playgroup. I want to observe the interactions between the children and the male helpers to find out how the men support and extend the children's learning. Their own observations will give us an additional view.

We have just finished a topic on 'ourselves'. I want to observe the children's play to see if the new activities, displays and resources have helped children develop more positive self images. I want to know if the children's parents can help me find out about the worthwhileness of our topic.

The toys and play materials in the toddler room have been arranged on new shelving. I want to observe how the children play with them to see if it offers them opportunities for filling and emptying, pairing and matching, fitting and taking apart. I may need to change the storage or add extra play things. My colleague, D, has offered to observe the three youngest children right through the session.

Nnu Ego was putting sand down drains today. I will observe her play tomorrow so that we can set up more challenging science materials in the outside play area which will help her explore the sand and water. And I must ask her mother about some of her experiences at home - she seems so engrossed in everything wet and watery.

I want to observe the effectiveness of the new room arrangement. Can Zoe reach the art materials from her wheelchair?

Mr Jones and Mrs Doherty on the management committee have asked to know more about our mathematics curriculum. This week we will focus our observations on this aspect of the children's play so that their records are up to date. I think we should take some photographs to illustrate the mathematical ideas that children explore in the brick corner. A picture of Fergus and his building of an ice-cream van would demonstrate his preoccupation with symmetry.

Yesterday Lynsi said she wouldn't touch the Black play people 'because they were dirty'. I was embarrassed, I didn't know what to say! We need to set up some observations of children's play with these toys so that we can support each other to develop more competent skills in challenging racist attitudes. Let's ask for some more training in this area. Some detailed observations could support our request for more training courses on challenging racism in childcare.

I shall use my observations of Fouzia when I meet her parents for a discussion tonight. They're worried about the clarity of her speech too, and they've been listening carefully at home.

Lee's play seemed so aimless, but after doing my target child observation over a morning session I can't wait to tell you all that I have seen. It all fits in with what his father told us last week about his interest in ladders.

MAKING TIME

A teamwork decision - whose time? and when?
Let's talk ...
Let's plan ...
OK by me ...
OK for you?

WHO WITH? (adults)

Observing alone?
Observing in pairs?
Observing with parents?
Observing with other specialists?   *WHY?*

WHO WITH? (children)

Children alone?
Children together?
Children playing with me?
Children playing without me?
Children's right to know?   *WHY?*

BEFORE I BEGIN

Do I need a checklist?
Name? Who needs to know?
Date? Confidentiality?
Age?
Date of birth?   *WHY?*

CHOOSING A SPOT

Where shall I observe?
Home? School?
Inside? Outside?
This area? That area?
In view? Out of view?   *WHY?*

HANDOUT 4B   **Starting points**

WHAT TECHNIQUE?

Words? Pictures?
Grids? Checklists?

(see also next activity)

WHY?

THE TOOLKIT

What things do I need?
Pens? Watch?
Notebooks?
Graphs?
Camera?
Shorthand code?

WHY?

WOW! THAT'S NEW

How will I respond to the unexpected? to a sudden
surprise?

Can I just keep quiet and watch?

Can I write it down even if I hadn't planned to observe?

HOW MUCH DETAIL?

How detailed shall I be?
I can't write everything?

WHY?

---

*Making
Assessment
Work*

OBSERVATIONS

to be negotiated - two or more sessions will be necessary

PREPARATION

Copies of the Handout **Selected techniques**, supplemented by the books referred to, if possible.

Handout 4B **I want to know,** from the previous activity.

This activity could last for weeks - or months! You will need to negotiate with the group how much time they want to allocate to trying out some observation techniques and evaluating their usefulness. This will probably depend on the previous experience of your group members. The minimum time would be about two hours, spread over two sessions.

INTRODUCTION TO THE ACTIVITY

In this activity you will be able to:

* try out some observation techniques

* evaluate their usefulness

Making Assessment Work

Activity 4C	Techniques

1. In small groups, look back at the Handout **I want to know.** Make a note of some aspect of a child (or children's) learning or development that you and your colleagues would like to know more about. Now use the Handout **Selected techniques** to help you decide on a method of observation that might help you find out what you 'want to know'.

2. In your workplace, practise this method of observation and bring your observation notes to the follow-up meeting.

3. At the subsequent meeting, work in a small group to evaluate your chosen technique. Think about what each technique has helped you to learn.

   - about a child (or children)

   - about your curriculum/workplace

   - about yourself

   - about doing observations

4. Repeat this sequence - of selection, practice, and evaluation - as appropriate for you and your group. This is a time to experiment - and to be critical of methods that will not support you in your work with young children. As part of the process of evaluation, you may want to turn back to the introduction to this section, which describes the power and purposes of observation.

1. TIME SAMPLING

In every group setting there is, at any one moment, too much going on for a single observer to be able to see it all. The observer, therefore, can only ever observe a selection of what is going on. In **Time sampling** the observer selects a child, or group of children, or activity, and notes down what is happening at pre-specified moments over a longer, substantial period.

For example:
Observations of the use of the water tray

> *Every 15 minutes over the whole morning session I will note down:*
>
> - *Who is present*
> - *What they are doing*
> - *What materials they are using*

Observations of Susan

> *How does she spend her mornings?*
> *Every ten minutes over the morning, I will note down:*
>
> - *Where she is*
> - *Who she is with*
> - *What she is doing and saying*

Observation of a group using the big blocks for an hour one morning

> *Every five minutes I will note down:*
>
> - *Who is talking*
> - *What s/he is saying (if possible)*

See also 'Joey' Handout 8A in Section Eight, **Making it work**, as an example of Time sampling in action.

HANDOUT 4C   **Selected techniques**

2. FREQUENCY SAMPLING

This is a different way of sampling events. The observer selects an aspect of behaviour of one or more children, and makes notes every time this particular behaviour occurs.

For example:
Observations of Khaleda

Every time I see her approach another person, adult or child, I will note down:

- Who she approaches
- How she initiates the interaction
- Her use of English or Bengali

Observations of Tom, William and Iqbal

Every time I see these three working together in an activity I will note down:

- What they are doing
- What they are saying
- Whether anyone else is involved

This observation technique gives you an accurate estimate of the **frequency** of certain behaviours. If used regularly, it can help you find out if the frequency is increasing or decreasing. You can use it to monitor progress, or something that concerns you, for individuals or for groups of children.

3. DURATION OBSERVING

This method allows you to establish how much time is actually spent by a child, or group of children, at a particular activity, or acting in a particular way.

For example:
Observations of Emma

Every time I see her isolated or separated from the group, apparently withdrawn into herself, I will note:

- the time and place
- how long she remains in this condition
- her general demeanour (eyes, face, body position)
- where she moves on to

For a fuller description of these three methods see Laishley J. *Working with Young Children* (1983) Arnold (Chapter 4).

4.16

OBSERVATIONS

HANDOUT 4C Contd   **Selected techniques**

4. FOCUSED OBSERVATION: WHAT DID THE CHILD(REN) ACTUALLY DO?

In this technique, you select an activity, or child, or group of children, about whom you wish to know more, and make detailed, on-the-spot, written notes of everything that happens. This intensive observation is very tiring and is best done in short bursts - five minutes on, five minutes off, for example, for an hour (or less) gives you a mass of information.

These observations are very useful in building up a full picture of children's understanding, their achievements and the challenges they face.

A fuller description can be found in Lally, M. (1991) *The Nursery Teacher in Action* Paul Chapman Publishing (Chapter 4) and in *Curriculum in Action: an approach to evaluation* (1981) P234 Open University publications (Unit Two Question One).

There is a fascinating and detailed description of this technique in practice by Michael Ruskin in Chapter 3, 'Observing Infants: Reflections on Methods' of *Closely Observed Infants* Miller, L. et al (eds) Duckworth (1989). The author describes a series of weekly observations made over a period of two years, focusing on the development of babies from the very earliest days. The observations all take place in the natural environment of the babies' homes, and there is an emphasis on the developing relationship between the babies, their mothers, and other intimate family members. The author discusses the way in which the observer's own emotional involvement in the process of mothering may affect the observations, the selection of evidence and the interpretations made.

5. TARGET CHILD OBSERVATIONS

This technique can be used when an individual child is the focus of interest or concern. By observing this child at regular, pre-set intervals throughout a session or sessions, a very full picture can be built up of his or her activities, interactions, and developing skills and understanding.

Before starting the observations, the observer may decide on a shorthand code so that the maximum of information can be recorded very quickly. The code might include initial letters for adults and other children, symbols for certain interactions (such as 'initiates talk', 'responds to question') and abbreviations for common activities.

For a full description, see Sylva, K. et al (1980) *Child Watching at Playgroup and Nursery School* Grant McIntyre (Appendix A), which gives details of a shorthand code and a grid on which to record information.

This method is also illustrated in Oates, J. (1991) *Working with Under Fives* PE 635 (The Competent Adult: developing observation skills). Open University publications.

6. AUDIOTAPES OF CHILDREN'S TALK

Children's talk, in conversation, discussion, imaginative play and story-telling, is so rich, and moves so fast, that it is impossible for an observer to note it all down as it happens. Audio or video tape recording is the only way to capture the fullness of what children say. Transcribing the tapes is very time-consuming, but the time is often well-spent, since being able to look back more than once at particular children's contributions gives the observer an unequalled insight into their thinking and learning.

A very full description of this approach, illustrating its power to illuminate the inner lives of young children, is given by Vivian Gussin Paley in each of her books about her kindergarten class, but especially in *Wally's Stories* (1987) and *The Boy Who Would Be a Helicopter* (1990), both published by Harvard University Press. This inspirational educator writes vividly in a narrative style, giving a fascinating and sensitive account of children's imaginative worlds, and her attempts, which are not always successful, to enter and understand them.

Some other observation techniques can be found in the books in the *Further Reading* listed at the end of this section (4.24).

ACTIVITY 4D   Descriptive observations

PREPARATION

1 hour 30 minutes

Copies of the Handout (or an overhead transparency)
Copies of some of the observations made in the previous activity

Notes to Group Leaders

In this activity your task is to encourage group members to challenge and support each other as they analyse the vocabulary they use for observing and assessing. You will help members to be both kind and ruthless to one another in thinking about some of the words they use in talking about their observations.

You will need to show group members the picture on the Handout, and do the first part of the discussion, before you give them the whole description of the activity.

INTRODUCTION TO THE ACTIVITY

This activity will help you learn about the ways in which you communicate your observations to others, and about the possible effects of the words you use on other people, and on the children themselves.

The purposes of the activity are for you to:

- distinguish between **descriptions, interpretations** and **judgements**

- think about the importance of making your descriptions as clear as you can, by avoiding jargon and buzz words

- think about the importance of making your descriptions as full as you can, using all your senses

- think about how your own emotions, and feelings remembered from childhood, may affect the judgements and interpretations you make.

Jane was naughty today

Making Assessment Work

1. As soon as you see the picture of Dorcas provided (on a handout or on an overhead transparency), jot down your initial responses, as quickly and as fully as you can. Then spend a few minutes comparing what you've written with one other person.

2. Different people may have seen different things. Some people will have noted **facts:**
'A child .....'
'The corner of a room .....'

Others will have made fuller **descriptions:**
'A little girl, covering her face with her hands, standing in the corner.'

You may also have made an **interpretation** of the picture, and, perhaps, a **judgement.**

For example:

INTERPRETATIONS	JUDGEMENTS
being punished	a mischievous child, she is such a scallywag a naughty girl, she was asking for that, that will teach her to mind her manners an undisciplined child, she needs limits set on her behaviour so that she can learn kind and courteous behaviour
playing hide and seek, counting to 100, ready or not!	a gregarious child, she can play collaboratively a clever child, she can count accurately a fortunate child, she has older siblings to show her how to play
feeling miserable	a sad child, she needs a cuddle a tearful child, she needs a tissue; a withdrawn child, she needs drawing in to the group a solitary child, she needs her own space to sort out her feelings a whiney child, she needs ignoring
And so on ...	

2. Work in a small group, thinking about the differences between description, interpretation and judgement. Why do people differ in the ways they describe, interpret, and judge what they see and hear? Is it because people have made a special study of one aspect of children's development? Is it because people interpret a child's behaviour in the light of their feelings about that child? Is it because their values and beliefs affect their judgements in different ways?

3. Spend a few minutes observing another person, giving a description of what you see, not an interpretation or a judgement.

    Work in pairs, taking it in turns to describe the body position of the person you are working with.
    Use as much descriptive language as you can. Watch out for feelings or opinions!
    For example, you might say:

    You are leaning back in your chair. Your left hand is lightly resting on your note pad and your right hand is circled under your chin. Your left leg is tucked underneath you and your right foot is hooked round the leg of the chair.

    Rather than:

    You seem very laid back and relaxed in the chair – have you really been listening? You look attentive, but perhaps that's just a mask. I think that your foot indicates that you are keen to hang on to your viewpoint. Have you tucked away your feelings as well as your leg?

    When each pair has given their descriptions, talk about the experience of trying to cut out interpretations and judgements. How did you respond to what you heard from your partner? How did it feel to be observed and described? Did you recognise yourself?

Talk about jargon!

They could mean anything!

I don't know what half of them mean!

My granny used to call me lively. She meant I was driving her mad

I can think of lots more. How about "Slow"

4.   When you describe children and the things they do, you do, of course, want to be clear, fair, and unprejudiced. But sometimes descriptive observations contain words that are judgements in themselves, or that might label a child in a damaging way.

For example:

Low IQ	quiet
unsettled home	withdrawn
attention seeking	aggressive
lack of motor coordination	disruptive
gifted	language problems
clingy	poor attention span
happy	hyperactive
naughty	behaviour problem
unstimulating home	language deprived

I was a quiet child – according to my teacher!

Look back at one of the observations you made in the last activity (**Techniques**). Work in pairs to note any words or phrases that remind you of words on this list, words that don't give a clear picture of what you actually saw, and what the children actually did.

Can you find descriptive words that are clearer? fairer? less judgemental?

Do your descriptions give you enough evidence for what you 'want to know'?

5.   Bring the discussion to a close by thinking about the implications of your work on this activity. Can you and your colleagues find ways of supporting each other in making full, fair, descriptive observations?

And the next time you say Susan's been uncooperative, I'll ask you to be clearer

All I meant was, she wouldn't do what I asked.

Oh!

I see what you mean ....

Making Assessment Work

about 45 minutes

PREPARATION

Pens and notebooks
Group members' notes on the observations they made in
Activity 4C **Techniques**
Copies of Handout 4B **I want to know**

Notes to Group Leaders

This activity concludes the group's work on this section. It will be an opportunity for you to support anyone who is finding this part of the pack difficult. You will want to emphasise that every group member is on a 'journey of learning', and that all educators face similar challenges. If the work on this section of the pack is to prove of value in the future, group members need to be encouraged to make realistic plans for development, confidently assess their present skills, and celebrate new areas of expertise.

INTRODUCTION TO THE ACTIVITY

As a conclusion to your work on **Observations**, in this activity you will

- review what you have learned in this section

- think about how to apply this learning in your workplace

Activity 4E   **What did we learn?**

1. Look back over the observations you made in Activity 4C, and work as a group to list the purposes of these observations. What did you hope to learn from them?

   Look back at the Handout you used in that activity, **I want to know,** which shows some educators' purposes in making observations. Do you use observations in any of these ways?

   Think back over the last few months in your workplace and add to your list any further purposes for which you used observation.

2. Now work in a smaller group of two or three to think about the whole range of your observation practice (with colleagues from your own workplace if possible).

   The following questions may help you to think about what you do now, and whether you need to make any changes.

TIME:
   how much time? when? who decides? does it just happen? is there time to discuss your observations?
   Is this good enough? Do you need to change?

TECHNIQUES:
   which do you use? which are most useful? in what ways?
   Is this good enough? Do you need to change?

PEOPLE:
   who is involved? staff? helpers? parents? children? why?
   Is this good enough? Do you need to change?

PURPOSES:
   does your practice match the purposes you listed earlier? if not, why not?
   Is this good enough? Do you need to change?

---

3. Work on your own to review your thinking and learning throughout this section. How can you apply this learning in your workplace, for the benefit of all concerned - children, parents and educators? Formulate one 'Good Resolution' that will help you put your learning to good use.

4. Come together in the large group to share your resolutions.

Review

The main themes of this section have been:

Observation is an essential and invaluable part of the work of early years educators, in whatever setting.

Observation means more than watching and listening; it is a process by which educators can understand and give meaning to what they see and hear, drawing on their own knowledge and experience, as well as on the evidence of their senses.

Observation means more than ticking off items on a checklist to establish efficiency or productivity; it enables educators to give a full and useful account of children's learning and development.

Observation means more than rating children's development on a numerical scale; observation reveals the richness and complexity of children's learning.

Observing children plays a crucial part in developing and monitoring a quality curriculum for all children.

REFERENCES

See titles given in Handout 4C **Techniques**

Hook, C. (1981) *Studying Classrooms* Deakin University Victoria

Hopkins, D. (1985) *A Teacher's Guide to Classroom Research* Open University Press

Holmes, A. & McMahon, L. (1978) *Learning from Observations* A guide to using 'Observing Children' in playgroup training and support Southern Region of Pre-School Playgroups, Reading

Moyles, J. (1989) *Just Playing: The Role and Status of Play in Early Childhood Education* Open University Press (Chapter 7)

Stonehouse, A. (ed) (1988) *Trusting Toddlers* Australian Early Childhood Association Canberra Publishing and Printing Co.

Tough, J. (1976) *Listening to Children Talking* Ward Lock Educational

Westmacott, E. V. A. & Cameron, R. J. (1981) *Behaviour Can Change* Macmillan Educational

Whitehead, M. (1980) 'First Words: The language diary of a bilingual child's early speach' See Reading B in Section Three **Looking at Learning**

SECTION 5
In search
of principles

5

INTRODUCTION TO THE SECTION

In the next section, **Principles into practice,** you will be able to look at some very practical questions about the practice of assessment - questions about who and how and when and where and what.

The purposes of this section are for you to:

* look at some general principles that underly assessment practice

* decide whether or not you agree with these principles

* consider which principles are most important to you

* explore the reasons **why** you think as you do

* examine your own practice to identify your own principles in action

There are three activities in this section. You are recommended to do all three. These three activities are most effective if carried out by members of a single staff group. Some of the trialling groups reported that they spent a whole day working together on this section, and you may want to consider this possibility.

This section leads directly into Section Six: **Principles into practice;** another possibility would be an inservice day or days for a staff group working on Sections Five and Six together.

Making Assessment Work

at least 1 hour 30 minutes -
see notes to group leaders below

ACTIVITY 5A   Do you agree?

PREPARATION

Copies of Handout 5A
Copies of sheets produced in
work on Section Three
Looking at learning (Activity 3D)

Notes to Group Leaders

The three activities in this section are very closely linked and form a coherent - and demanding - whole. You may want to explore the possibility of using them at a full day in-service meeting for your staff group. If you use the activities at separate sessions, be sure to allow plenty of time for members to support and sustain each other's thinking around some difficult and complex issues.

INTRODUCTION TO THE ACTIVITY

In this activity you will:

• examine critically some statements about assessment

• decide whether you agree with these statements

• think about which statements are most important to you in your work with young children

ACTIVITY 5A   Do you agree?

1. Working on your own, use the grid on the Handout provided to show whether you agree or disagree with some simple statements about assessment that have been taken from documents produced in a variety of early years settings.

2. Work with three or four other people to compare and discuss what you have marked on the grid. Try to find out whether you all mean the same by certain key words (for example, curriculum, relationships, involved ....)

3. In the same group, work right through the list of principles with which you agree, identifying the ones that, as a group, you want to establish as the basis for your assessment practice. You may need to change the wording of the statements on the grid, so that they say exactly what you want them to say. Refer back to the statements you made about learning in Activity 3D, to check for consistency in your approach.

4. As each small group works through the list, it will be necessary for the whole staff group to come together from time to time, to check on the progress of the different discussions. It is worth allowing plenty of time for this process, however long it takes, since it is an opportunity for you all to agree on your underlying principles.

5. By the end of the session, you will, as a staff group, have established the key principles that will shape your assessment practice. You will have agreed on the precise wording of the principles that you stand for, and you will all have had the opportunity to check out that you share a common understanding of what you have agreed.

Do you agree?	Strongly agree	Agree	Disagree	Strongly disagree
1 Parents are providers as well as receivers of information and must be involved in the assessment process.				
2 All the adult staff should be involved in the process of assessment.				
3 Children should be involved in the assessment of their own progress and development.				
4 We should only assess those aspects of children's learning and development that we believe to be truly important.				
5 To assess effectively we need to be certain of the kinds of learning that we value most.				
6 Assessments of children of nearly school age should match the assessment practices used by the school as the children enter Key Stage One of the National Curriculum.				
7 Records should show the development of each child's social relationships and his/her attachments to key people.				
8 Assessment must be based on detailed observations of what children do and say.				
9 Written records should include factual evidence, sensitive interpretations and tentative judgements.				
10 Written records should not show isolated incidents but selected observations that demonstrate progress and development.				
11 When appropriate, assessments of bilingual children should be made in the child's home language by a person who knows about the child's cultural heritage.				
12 Assessment must take account of the possible effects of the context on the child (for example, the language used, the child's previous experience, the child's emotional state).				
13 Assessments of individual children should be used in planning activities for those children.				
14 Assessments made over a period of time should be used to review and evaluate the provision made for the children during that time.				
15 Parents need time to talk about what they **feel** as well as about what they **know** before making decisions about what to do next for the benefit of **their** child.				
16 Please add some more......				
17 ......of your own				

| ACTIVITY 5B | Looking for reasons |

PREPARATION

List of principles agreed during Activity 5A

Copies of Handout 5B

at least 1 hour, or possibly longer, if used during an in-service day

Notes to Group Leaders

This activity depends on the persistent use of 'why?' questions. You may need to encourage some group members to put some pressure on each other, firmly and gently, through their questions.

At the end of work on this section, group members will have produced two lists - a list of principles (5A) and a list of beliefs (5B). They will need both these lists for work on Section Six **Principles into practice.**

INTRODUCTION TO THE ACTIVITY

In ordinary everyday life, we don't need to ask ourselves WHY about many of our choices and preferences. No-one has ever asked me WHY I like gooseberries and I have never worried about it.

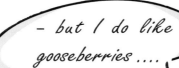

- but I do like gooseberries ....

But in looking for ways of going about the process of assessment, we do need to be clear about the reasons for our decisions .... 'I like it!' is a perfectly acceptable way of responding to a bowl of gooseberries - but it isn't enough when we're looking at approaches to children's learning.

In this activity you will be able to

- explore the reasons behind some of your principles

- think about **why** you give these reasons for your principles

- keep asking yourself ..... but why?

Making Assessment Work

IN SEARCH OF PRINCIPLES

1. Working in a small group, if possible the same group as in the previous activity (5A), look back at the list of principles that you agreed on together.

2. Now take one idea at a time and start to ask each other WHY this principle is important to you.

    Use the Handout provided to record your thinking.

    Write the key words from the idea you're working with on the left hand side of the page (under the **Start here** sign).

    For example, you might choose to look more closely at the principle of 'involving children in the process of assessment'.

    So on the left hand side, write: 'involving children.' Now, in the next column, list all the possible reasons why you want to involve children. What would you achieve by it?

    In the next column, ask yourselves some questions about the reasons you have listed. **Why** do these reasons make your case convincing?

    In the last column, write the answers to your own questions - which won't necessarily be easy to answer.

    Please feel free to add more '**But why?**' and '**Because**' columns of your own.

3. You may need to repeat this process more than once for each key idea, and each reason behind the reason.

    But sooner or later you will get to a point where you feel you can't go any further.

    You will have reached a point where you can say quite firmly: 'This is what I believe - and I'm sticking to it!'

    Try to find a form of words - a phrase or sentence - that expresses this basic belief of yours - about
    children
                or **learning**
                            or **parents**
                                        or **your colleagues**
                                                    or .....

and list them here:

I firmly believe ....

....

....

....

This list is rather different from the list of principles you agreed on in the first activity. You have moved on from there, to an understanding of the reasons behind your principles. You will need both lists in your work on the next section, **Principles into practice,** so keep them in a safe place.

Making Assessment Work

HANDOUT 5B **Looking for reasons**

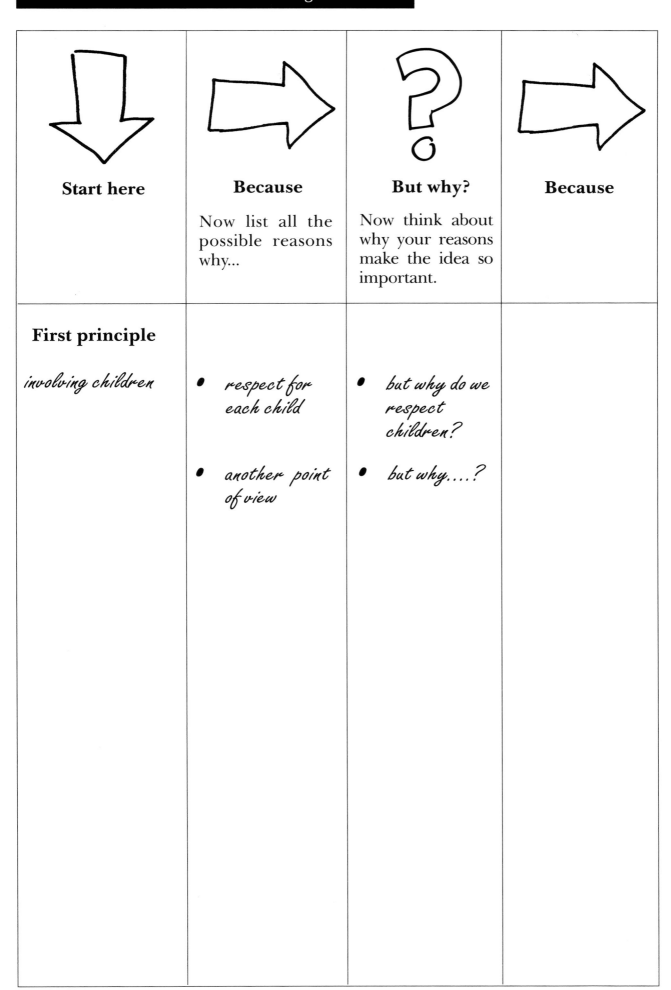

Start here	Because	But why?	Because
	Now list all the possible reasons why...	Now think about why your reasons make the idea so important.	
First principle *involving children*	• *respect for each child* • *another point of view*	• *but why do we respect children?* • *but why....?*	

about 30 minutes

ACTIVITY 5C	From practice to principle

PREPARATION

Copies of the list of principles agreed in Activity 5A:
Do you agree?

BEFORE THE MEETING

Select an example of the assessment practice in your own workplace and bring it to the meeting.

Notes to Group Leaders

This activity depends on a critical review of group members' own practice. You may need to encourage people to steer carefully between being uncritically cosy and being destructive. Stressing the confidentiality of the group may help members feel secure enough to be self critical.

INTRODUCTION TO THE ACTIVITY

Now that you have established the important principles that you believe should underly your assessment practice, you will want to check back with what actually happens in your workplace.

In this activity you will

- select one aspect of your current assessment practice

- identify the principle or principles on which it is based

ACTIVITY 5C   From practice to principle

1.   Working in a small group, describe the example you have brought of part of your assessment practice. Answer your colleagues' questions about how, when, and where you use the check-list, record card, note-book, folder - or whatever you have brought.

2.   Look back at the list of principles you agreed in Activity 5A, and try to identify which of these principles are expressed in the practice you have described.

     In effect, you will be asking yourself:
     '**Why** do we do it like this?'

3.   When everyone in the group has had a chance to talk about a particular piece of assessment practice, spend a little time reflecting on what you have learned about the connection between principles and practices.

Review

SECTION FIVE: IN SEARCH OF PRINCIPLES

The main themes of this section have been:

in assessment, we express some firmly held but sometimes unarticulated principles

- about children
- about learning
- about parents and educators

in effective assessment, we can articulate these principles clearly and confidently

in effective assessment we assess those aspects of children's learning and development that we believe to be truly important

in effective assessment we draw on what we know about the beneficial effects of involving parents and children in the process

in effective assessment we draw on what we know about the possibly damaging effects of the context of assessment

in effective assessment, our understanding of children's learning, supported by our careful, systematic observations, is used to enrich and extend the curriculum we offer.

FURTHER READING

Athey, C. (1989) *Extending Thought in Young Children*. Paul Chapman Publishing

Blenkin, G. and Kelly, V. (1992) *Assessment in Early Childhood Education*. Paul Chapman Publishing

Donaldson, M. (1984) *Children's Minds*. Fontana

Drummond M. J. (1993) *Assessing Children's Learning*, David Fulton Press

Drummond, M. J. and Nutbrown, C. (1992) 'Assessing Young Children's Learning' in Pugh G (ed) *Contemporary Issues in the Early Years*. Paul Chapman Publishing

SECTION 6
Principles into practice

6

Making
Assessment
Work

SECTION SIX   PRINCIPLES INTO PRACTICE

INTRODUCTION

In this section, you will be able to start building on the ground you cleared in Section Five **In search of principles.**

The purpose of this section are for you to:

* make some practical decisions about assessment in your own workplace

* generate some questions of how, who, what and when to help you make these decisions

* and, first, express some of the doubts and anxieties that may be in your mind

There is a short introductory activity to this section, followed by one substantial, very practical activity, which is most suitable for use by a staff group, or by educators from very similar settings.

This whole section is probably most useful if it forms part of an in-service training day for a staff group or groups, following on closely, probably on the same day, from work on the previous section **In search of principles.**

20 minutes

| **ACTIVITY 6A** | **It's all very well but ....** |

PREPARATION

Pens and notebooks

INTRODUCTION TO THE ACTIVITY

Sometimes there's quite a difference between what people say and what they really think. It's easy to get carried away by the discussion that's going on out loud, and to assume that everybody really does agree. In reality, there may be a lot of doubt and anxiety in people's minds, which they don't feel free to talk about without encouragement.

In this activity you will be able to:

- express some of your anxieties

- think about possible difficulties in your work so that you are better prepared to overcome them.

UNSPOKEN THOUGHTS ....

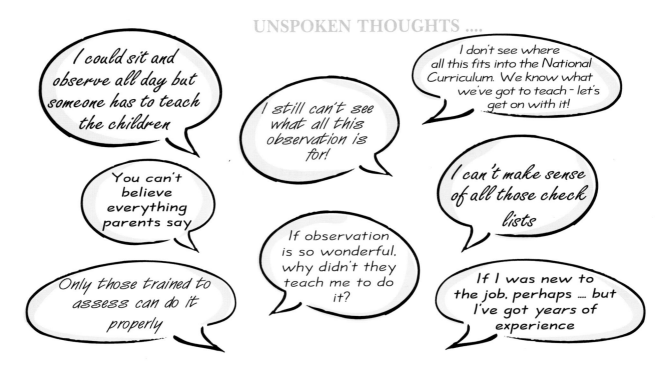

1. Working on your own, make a few jotted notes of some of your unspoken thoughts, some of your concerns, about the difficult issues you are working on in this pack.

2. Work with one other person to discuss what you have written. Remind each other that it is perfectly normal to feel anxious and concerned about the things that are important to you. Reassure each other that, at your best, you can talk yourselves out of seeing nothing but doubts and difficulties. In fact, knowing what difficulties lie ahead may help you, in the long run, to work more effectively to overcome them.

ACTIVITY 6B   Getting down to it

PREPARATION

Copies of the list of principles agreed
in Activity 5A **Do you agree?**

Copies of the Handout

at least one hour, or
preferably longer, if
used as part of a
staff training day

After so much discussion at an abstract level during
Section Five, it will be important to support group
members as they turn their attention to the nitty-
gritty practicalities of everyday routines. They may
need encouragement to discuss at such a mundane
level, using proper names (for 'Who?' questions)
and concrete nouns (for 'Where?' questions) for
example. Your task is to help them appreciate that
the effectiveness of a system of assessment does, in
reality, depend not just on the principles that
underly it, but also on the practical details that
make it happen. So that where to keep the children's
on-going records, for example, may be a crucially
important question in the development of good
practice, even though it might sound superficial at
first.

INTRODUCTION TO THE ACTIVITY

Now it is time to start making decisions about the actual practice
of assessment. To help you do this, in the activity you will:

- select one principle to work on in detail

- identify 'how', 'what', 'when' and 'where' questions
  to help you discuss the down-to-earth details

- work on answering, in concrete terms, the
  questions you have set yourselves

*Making
Assessment
Work*

1. Working in a small group, select one of the principles on your list from your work on the last section, and write it in the space provided for it on the handout.

2. Now imagine that you and your colleagues have actually achieved the challenge of putting this principle into practice. Think about all the different decisions you would have taken on your way to this achievement.

Use these question words to help you think about these decisions:

Who?   What?   How?   What if?   Where?   When?

3. For example, one group of educators working with the trial version of this pack worked on the principle:

> Assessment should be used to review
> and evaluate the provision made
> for the children

They identified a number of questions to help them think about ways of putting this principle into action.

 **Who?**
makes these assessments anyway?
do we share them with?
is in the best position to make sure we don't breach our confidentiality agreements?

 **What?**
sorts of assessments will we select for this purpose?
should be the priority in our review and evaluation?

 **How?**
do we keep parents informed of what we are doing?
do we preserve a sense of balance?
can we involve parents in this process?

 **When?**
do we start?
do we stop?

 **Where?**
will we find the staff time for the discussion we will need?

*Making
Assessment
Work*

4.   When you have generated a list of Who - When - What ....
     questions, work in the same groups, using your list of
     questions as the starting point for a very down-to-earth
     discussion about the practicalities of assessment. Make
     sure that someone takes notes of your discussion, (taking
     it in turns if the discussion is a long one), so that you can
     review your work in the next activity.

     You will probably find that for each of your questions
     there are several possibilities to be considered. Keep a
     note of the different possibilities as you discuss them
     and, if possible, some of the comments made. For
     example, a group discussing the principle of using
     the assessment of an individual to review provision for
     that child, asked themselves:

'How often will the record be added to?'

POSSIBILITIES	COMMENTS
Every day?	Have a heart! with 26 children!!
Once a week?	A bit more realistic
Once a month?	You might miss something important
On a rota system?	It's a bit mechanical isn't it?
When you see something significant?	Yes, that sounds good, but you might overlook some children

...... And so on ......

---

5.   This discussion could take a very long time. Don't feel you
     have to settle everything in one session. It may be better
     to do some work on this activity at more than one meeting,
     especially if there are three or four principles that you want
     to put into practice. Keep notes of your discussion,
     including the possibilities that you leave open, as well as
     the firm decisions that you make.

     You will probably find the work you did in other sections
     of the pack useful. The work on observation techniques in
     Section Four for example, may be helpful when you tackle
     How? and When? questions.

6.   At the end of your work on this activity, come together as
     a group to review your discussion as a whole. You will be
     able to decide on your priorities in putting all your
     thinking into practice in your own workplace.

Making
Assessment
Work

Who?

When?

Where?

What?

How?

Write the principle you're going to work on in here.
Now think about the small questions that will help you recognise this principle in practice.

Question 1 ....
....
....
Question 2 ....
....
....
Question 3 ....
....
....
Question 4 ....
....
....
Question 5 ....
....
....
Question 6 ....
....
....
Question 7 ....
....
....
Question 8 ....
....
....

SECTION SIX: PRINCIPLES INTO PRACTICE

The main themes of this section have been:

principles are important, but what we actually do is just as important

to make our principles effective, we must develop practices that match them

it is important to be able to see and explain the connections between our principles and our practices

As in Section Five.

SECTION 7
Writing
it down

INTRODUCTION

Writing it down is another stage in the process of Making Assessment Work. It is essential to have worked through Sections One to Six of this pack before you begin to think about written records. It may be tempting to start here if you are under pressure to account for your observation and assessment practice. You may want to have written evidence to share with parents, or to show to 'the boss' or the governors. It is easy to rush into getting it down on paper before giving enough time to consider the purposes of assessment. It may be difficult to make thoughtful or informed choices about the format of your written records if you have not made time to think about the issues raised by the activities in the previous sections.

You will start your work on this section by looking at how other educators go about 'writing it down'. However, no assessment format can be right for your staff group until you have evaluated it, according to your values and principles. You will need to adapt your chosen format to fit in with what you believe, so that it will reflect your ways of working with children.

The purposes of this section are for you to:

- review and evaluate examples of other educators' written records of their observations and assessments

- select 'headings' for your records that reflect the curriculum in your workplace (what you do and say, and all that children do, say, know, feel and learn)

- ensure that all the aspects of children's development and learning that you plan for in your workplace are reflected in the format you choose

- create or update **your own** format for assessment, for your children, to be used by **your** staff team, with the parents of the children in **your** workplace

There are two activities (both essential) in this section, and the second follows on directly from the first. However, the second activity is most suitable for use by a staff group from the same workplace, so that if the group members all work in different settings, the activity will need to be slightly adapted.

Making Assessment Work

to be negotiated with
group members

*Making
Assessment
Work*

ACTIVITY 7A   Tried and tested

PREPARATION

Handouts 7A1-5

The set of principles for assessment developed by group members in Activity 5A.

One week before ask members to prepare their own assessment formats to use in this activity (see below).

BEFORE THE MEETING

Group members to bring their own assessment formats (where appropriate).

Notes to Group Leaders

Group members will be asked to bring examples of their own assessment formats. They will need to bring a page of explanations or introduction, and a filled-in example as well as a blank one. Some members of the group may not have developed their own formats, or they may not feel confident enough to share them with the group. Group members new to written assessments will begin with the Handouts provided in the pack. Whether group members are new to working on assessment, or whether they have strongly established traditions in their workplace, you will need to create an atmosphere where each member feels that their learning is being supported, that each has something to learn. Group members whose long established practice has given them confidence and certainty may need to be challenged, so that their formats can be extended, updated or revised to accommodate the principles established in Activity 5A. Group members who are drawing up systematic formats of assessment for the first time will need support to get started.

It is difficult to estimate how long this activity will take. It will depend on the group members' experience, and on how much they need to revise or extend their record keeping practice.

ACTIVITY 7A　　　　　Tried and tested

INTRODUCTION TO THE ACTIVITY

In this activity you will look at different ways of writing down observations and assessments. The examples provided have been selected to illustrate different views of curriculum, and different approaches to learning; they have been developed by educators working in different settings. They are extracts, rather than complete record-systems, but they will give you a starting point for the activities that follow. You will be able to think about the benefits and the disadvantages of each method. The extracts will help you choose your own way of recording, or they may offer you ideas to incorporate into your present system. You are invited to include an example of your own system for 'writing it down' as one of the examples for discussion.

The purpose of this activity is for you to:

* review and evaluate examples of how other educators make written records of their observations and assessments of children's development and learning.

The following examples are provided:

> An observation sheet using knowledge of children's schematic development to make and analyse observations (Handout 7A1)
>
> The Child Anecdotal Record from a High/Scope nursery class, based on key learning experiences (Handout 7A2)
>
> Playladders: a method of observing how children play; these observations are used to help the child reach the next step on a ladder of development (Handout 7A3)
>
> 'All About Me': a record of development written in the first person, to be filled in by parents and other educators, to enable discussion of a child's progress - a here-and-now snapshot of many aspects of a child's development for children aged two to six (Handout 7A4)
>
> The Primary Language Record: a format for recording the language development of children used in nursery and primary school classrooms (Handout 7A5)

Making Assessment Work

1 Working alone, read the five examples provided of 'writing it down'. Please include an example of your own system of record-keeping if this is appropriate.

2. In small groups of three or four examine critically each of these different methods of record keeping. The following questions may help you to evaluate their usefulness to you.

- What is your first impression of each method? Does it seem to fit with your way of working?

- If there are parts of each method that you feel very positively about, ask yourself or each other: Why?

- If there are parts of each method that you feel uncomfortable with, ask yourself and each other: Why?

- To what extent are parents involved in each method of record-keeping?

- Is there scope to involve the children themselves, where appropriate?

- Is the format suitable for all children, whatever their special learning needs or abilities?

- Is the format sensitive to the cultural heritage and the variety of languages of the children and the families you work with?

- Does the format reflect a curriculum that is appropriate for the children you work with? In what ways?

3. Select the two formats that seem to be most appropriate for you in your workplace. Working in pairs, make a list of your reasons for selecting these two, including any reservations you may have. Be sure to keep asking each other Why?, so that you are both clear about the reasons for your judgements.

4. Use the set of principles that you developed in Section Five as another means of evaluating your selected examples. Do these formats express the principles that are at the heart of effective assessment for you? If there is a mismatch between practice and principle you may need to reconsider. (During the trialling of this pack one group discovered they had selected a format that did not agree with any of their principles. After recovering from the shock, they went back to the drawing board!)

5. As a whole group, share your evaluation of these formats for 'writing it down'. Don't forget to include an evaluation of the match between your principles and these particular practices.

Making Assessment Work

Cathy Nutbrown
Area Coordinator - Early Childhood Education
City of Sheffield Education Department

USING KNOWLEDGE OF CHILDREN'S SCHEMATIC DEVELOPMENT TO MAKE AND ANALYSE OBSERVATIONS

Chris Athey's work on young children's schematic development can help us to understand the intellectual development of young children.

Young children, from birth, demonstrate some schemas (repeatable pattern of behaviour and thought), such as sucking and grasping. Later schemas seem to increase in number and complexity and become linked and coordinated.

The Froebel Early Childhood Project (Athey 1990) identified children's schemas and worked to nourish and extend them through a wide range of experiences, which formed a quality curriculum for young children. The experiences offered represented an attempt to fit the curriculum to the predominant schematic interests of the child. An important element of work with schemas in mind is fitting the curriculum to each child, rather than making all children fit the same curriculum.

The children in Chris Athey's project made highly significant gains in IQ and other standardised tests. These gains may be attributed to matching curriculum content to a child's schema, and to the involvement of parents who worked with their child, identified the child's schemas, and then supported their development.

For example, a child exploring objects that rotate might have a predominant interest in rotation and circular objects. This is called a 'dynamic circular' schema. The curriculum content to nourish this pattern of interest and thought might include a visit to a working water-wheel, watching tyres being changed on a vehicle, using a drill or a vice on a woodwork bench. These experiences contain opportunities for mathematical, scientific and linguistic learning, which are essential features of any nursery curriculum.

The early years educator can, through observation, identify a child's schematic interest and nourish it with worthwhile curriculum content. Matching curriculum to child can promote a child's motivation and development.

Observations are needed of all children to identify their predominant schemas, and to help to plan further experiences. Worthwhile experiences that are planned to match particular schemas can also be valuable for children whose schemas have not been identified.

The observation sheet given below has been completed for a four-year-old child who seems to have a predominant vertical schema. The sheet makes it possible to analyse the child's learning and to plan further action. Dates and initials of the worker are useful for checking, reflecting and asking for more information at a later date. This sheet can form part of a child's accumulating record.

Using schemas as a focus for observations ensures that children's actions are recorded, learning identified and a curriculum planned to match.

OBSERVATION SHEET

NAME *Danika, Age Four*

OBSERVATION	ANALYSIS OF LEARNING	ACTION	DATE & INITIALS
Following a visit to some flats, D made a construction of cardboard boxes, piling one on top of another using a chair to reach.	Motor and symbolic representation of vertical schema. Work on 'higher' and 'lower'. Introducing vocabulary using appropriate material.	Move into counting boxes. Stabilising structure. More experience of vertical e.g. lifts and escalators.	CN 6.9.91
D. on the climbing frame. Sliding down the slide. She said 'Going down' 'Going up'. Rolling cars and dolls down the slope.	Experimenting with forces and gravity.	More experiences of slopes and rolling experiences. Timing how long it takes to go down.	CN 14.9.91
D. drew a picture. Lots of //// lines. 'This is water falling out of the sky', 'It comes down and goes in the puddles,' D. said.	Understanding early scientific notions of rain and the environment.	Maybe provide different kinds of pouring tools. Showerhead, watering can to encourage observation. Feed in appropriate language.	CN 17.9.91
D's mum reported that D. is going to the top of the stairs and watching a ball bounce to the bottom. She's concerned.	Experiencing gravity and forces again.	Need to provide acceptable safe experiences for observing, bouncing and dropping objects.	CN 25.9.91

WRITING IT DOWN

OBSERVATION SHEET

NAME _____

OBSERVATION	ANALYSIS OF LEARNING	ACTION	DATE & INITIALS

WRITING IT DOWN

Pam Lafferty, Teacher in Charge - Stokenchurch Nursery Oxford, and High/Scope Development Officer

For more information about the High/Scope Curriculum and Key Experiences contact High/Scope UK, Copperfield House, 190-192 Maple Road, Penge, London SE 20 8HT Tel: 081 676 0220

A PERSONAL EXPERIENCE

Stokenchurch Nursery is a 39 place Nursery class for children attending on a part time basis; the staff consists of a teacher and two nursery nurses. We work on a 1:13 ratio but this is usually supplemented by parents, students and welfare assistants. The welfare assistants are employed on an hourly basis when we have children with special needs.

It had always been part of our daily pattern to talk about what happened during the session, referring to specific incidents involving children and things they said, but this information was not written down.

During my course of High/Scope training I became aware of the High/Scope Child Anecdotal Record (C.A.R.). It seemed an easy and logical step for us at this time to begin using it. At first this was a very haphazard and random collection of observations and a lot of discussion around where to put it and how to write it on the C.A.R. sheet. We spent about 15 minutes doing this and collected about six/eight observations. Gradually as the sheets built up they began to show us a very personal picture of how each child was progressing in all areas of the curriculum, and for ourselves we felt we had a much more in-depth knowledge of each child. We usually keep a notebook and pencil with us to write things down as they happen.

The sheets are used in a variety of ways for:

- sharing with parents in an on-going dialogue about how their children are developing

- planning together as a staff team, and deciding what areas of learning experiences should be focused on

- planning for individual children

- pinpointing 'hidden children' who can then be observed more closely

- pinpointing 'hidden' areas of the curriculum which can then be discussed and reviewed

- seeing changes in a child and how particular interests develop

- reducing assumptions and inferences through objective observations

Making Assessment Work

We have found in using them that they have increased our knowledge and understanding of children's learning, and given us a stronger sense of purpose in our planning and development.

CHILD ANECDOTAL RECORD IN THE HIGH/SCOPE CURRICULUM

The following criteria could help in the development of effective record-keeping:

Quick to complete   Records are more likely to be kept up to date if a regular short amount of time can be allocated to complete them.

Easy to understand   This is especially important when the records may be passed on to a variety of settings.

Useful   Records serve as the starting points for the educators both in the child's present setting, and in the next.

Relevant   Records can show a selection of information with a specific focus.

Objective   Records need to be factual, focusing on what children do and say, avoiding assumptions and inferences.

The High/Scope assessment and record keeping sheet (C.A.R.) meets all of these criteria, and can be used in a variety of settings. Whilst interacting with the children throughout the session, the adults jot down what children are doing and saying. The focus of these anecdotal observations will have been decided before the session. At a later time the adults meet together to discuss their observations and record them on individual C.A.R. sheets. The headings on the sheets correspond to the High/Scope Key Experiences* and cover all areas of children's learning and development.

The positive points about these record-sheets are:

• they are done daily but not for each child

• they are quick to complete - 10/15 minutes per day

• they focus on what the child has done or said

• they focus on where the child is in his/her development

• they are done as a team

• they help in filling in local authority or other records

*The High/Scope Key Experiences are central to children's learning and development. The High/Scope curriculum is based on providing these key experiences for all children, and on ensuring that the principle of 'active learning' is paramount throughout their experiences.

Pam Lafferty 1992
High/Scope Endorsed Trainer

Child's Name: *Jimmie*

HIGH/SCOPE EDUCATIONAL RESEARCH FOUNDATION

Child Anecdotal Record (C.A.R.)

Birth Date: 16/9/86

(a condensed sheet for the purposes of this publication)
Remember to date all entries

CLASSIFICATION	CREATIVE REPRESENTATION	SERIATION	NUMBER
7/10/91 - Stacked up the brick piles into separate colours - red, blue, green and yellow	2/9/91 - Playing with the plastic animals and making the appropriate sounds for horse, cow and pig	11/9/91 - Remarked that the new fruit bowl was heavier than the old one	18/9/91 - Said "a few means not a lot"
12/11/91 - Said "My boots are red and yours are blue"	24/9/91 - Nailed two pieces of wood together in a cross shape and said it was an aeroplane	27/9/92 - Comparing paint brushes said "Mine's larger and fatter than yours"	18/11/91 - Cut dough into four pieces and said "I've made four cakes"
6/12/91 - Looking at the words "Jack" and "Jake" said that the two names were nearly the same, just a little bit different.	8/11/91 - Drew a robin with minute details and coloured it in accurately with red brown and white.	17/12/91 - Chose a number of triangle shapes from the box and arranged them in order of increasing size	6/12/91 - Counted seven penguins accurately on a friend's jumper

LANGUAGE AND LITERACY		MUSIC AND MOVEMENT	SOCIAL RELATIONS/ INITIATIVE
3/9/91 - Said "go jo flo blow - they sound the same"		12/9/91 - Was walking around the nursery on all fours swaying from side to side being an elephant	4/10/91 - On coming from the garden to the inside, stopped in the doorway to leave muddy wellingtons outside
5/9/91 - J. was sitting looking at a story book and telling a story from the pictures		21/10/91 - For the first time managed to use her legs to make the swing go	29/10/91 - Took a friend into the bathroom and used a cotton wool ball to wipe mud from his knee
3/12/91 - Whilst sitting on a toilet seat said that she was sitting on an "o"		13/12/91 - Used scissors to cut a "fringe" along the side of a piece of paper	12/12/91 - At snack time said "G only likes bananas - please save one for him"

SPACE	TIME		
23/9/91 - Talking to another child about a hat said "you need the ribbons at the back, not the side"	8/10/91 - When the tidy-up sound was made J. began to put things from the floor into their correct baskets		
30/10/91 - Folded a piece of card in half to form a tunnel and then walked plastic animals through it and used the word "through"	28/11/91 - Said "If you want to find me later, I'll be in the Book Area"		
9/12/91 - Noticed a triangular patch of light on the carpet and found a triangle shape to fit exactly on top of it	29/11/91 - Looked at a list of names on the board and said "It will be Matthew's turn to open the door tomorrow"		

WRITING IT DOWN

HIGH/SCOPE CHILD ANECDOTAL RECORD - KEY EXPERIENCES FOR CHILDREN AGE 3 TO 5

Child's Name:

Remember to date all entries

Language and literacy	Classification	Creative representation	Seriation	Space	Number	Time	Music and movement	Social relations/ Initiative

Hannah Mortimer
Educational Psychologist
North Yorkshire L.E.A.

'Playladders' can be obtained by sending a cheque for £1.50 to Hannah Mortimer, Ainderby Hall, Northallerton, North Yorkshire DL7 9QJ. Parts of the booklet are illustrated in this handout.

PLAYLADDERS

Playladders are checklists of young children's play as they go about their activities in nursery, playgroup or at home. They are a method of observing and recording how a child plays now, and they provide ideas on how to help the child reach the next step. 'Playladders' combine the step-by-step approach developed in special education, with the practicalities of what goes on in a busy playroom.

The Playladders booklet contains 21 playladders, each one representing an activity typically available for under fives, for example: climbing frames, painting, home corner, book corner or glue table. Each activity is broken down into progressive steps and skills. The emphasis is on flexibility, and users are encouraged to adapt, modify or add to the ladders to suit the particular child, culture and setting. There are also blank playladders to build up for yourself.

Playladders were originally designed for nursery and playgroup staff who had children with special educational needs in their classes.

Playladders provide the ideas for moving one step at a time from simple to more complex play, encouraging young children in their learning.

AN EXAMPLE OF THE PLAYLADDERS IN USE

Beth was a three-year-old who had just started at her local nursery class. At first, she was very quiet and spent the entire session walking up and down the room pushing a trolley. She resisted any advances from the adults and children. We used the Playladders to map her play; this needed a lot of help from her mother as Beth did so little for us in nursery. Together we concluded that Beth was still at an early stage in all areas of her play and social life, and that pushing a trolley was her safest option in her new and unfamiliar setting.

One of us began to befriend Beth, who gradually allowed the contact. She began to seek this helper out and would park her trolley for a moment while watching other children play, so long as the helper was nearby. She would help to clear up using her trolley and, in time, park it long enough to draw a scribble which she then carried around in it. Using the Playladders for ideas, and the trolley as a starting point, Beth gradually increased her repertoire of play and felt safe to leave her trolley and join in.

POSTSCRIPT

If you don't work in a playgroup, but in some other kind of setting, don't be tempted to dismiss this format out of hand. It can readily be adapted for other settings. For example, during the trialling of the pack, this format was developed by a junior school teacher into a complete record-keeping system for children's progress in physical education.

playladders

name: Beth   age 3

nursery area: "LET'S PRETEND" AREA

play activity: Home Corner

step	repertoire	
3	Combines play with other areas of the nursery (e.g. uses art work to decorate, makes model cooker etc.) Joins in fully with other children in imaginative plays using own imaginative ideas.	✓
2	Collects pans for pan cupboard, food for pantry, etc. Joins in a game directed by other children. — No Puts dolly to bed and covers it up. — mob-hats Dresses and undresses dolly. Plays on own with more complicated etc. activity (moving from one part of home corner to another) e.g. making breakfast.. Plays on own; simple activity e.g. ironing. Holds imaginary phone conversation. ✗	
1	Puts things in and out of kitchen cupboards. Helps to tidy up. — trolley! Brings adult a "cup of tea" if asked. Holds and cuddles doll. Kisses doll if adult suggests it. ✗ Replies to adults on phone. ✗ Speaks into phone held by adult. ✗ ↯↯↯↯↯ Plays very silently	

---

playladders

name: Beth   Age 3

nursery area: Large space

play activity: trolley   our plan for the trolley!

step	repertoire	
3	Will play imaginatively with trolley and another child. Will join in an activity with trolley with another child. Will freely leave trolley for another activity.	✓
2	Will allow another child to borrow trolley when busy (adult help?) ✓ Will "park" trolley to do a short activity ✓ Will carry toys in has trolley	
1	Will keep tidy up with trolley ✓ Will stop pushing trolley to watch other children ✗ Will allow adult to put something in trolley ✗ Pushes trolley ✗	

playladders

name:
nursery area:
play activity:

step	repertoire	✓
3		
2		
1		

playladders

name:
nursery area: "LET'S PRETEND" AREA
play activity: Dressing Up

step	repertoire	✓
3	Combines with other activities e.g. spaceman on climbing frame adopted as rocket. Selects clothes to suit an imaginary idea. ("These'll do for .....") Combines into a game (e.g. playing witches) Makes own props to go with outfit e.g. space helmet.	
2	Manages most clothes without help. Speaks as if a different person. Has own ideas and asks for help to develop them. Combines dressing up with simple props e.g. wand. Selects clothes for an idea provided by adult e.g. witch, giant.	
1	Selects special clothers for special activities e.g. apron. Asks for help e.g. with apron. Allows self to be dressed up. Tries on hats or shoes. Admires self in mirror	

Professor Sheila Wolfendale
Polytechnic of East London

Wolfendale, S. (1990) *All About Me*, NES Arnold, Ludlow Hill Road, West Bridgford, Nottingham NG2 6HD. Price £3.95

ALL ABOUT ME

All About Me is a checklist that enables parents to note down and record from time to time their child's development and progress. It is a record for the family, and it gives parents a basis on which to discuss their child's progress with a teacher in nursery or infant class, a nursery worker, or a playgroup leader. It was first tried out with over 130 children from all over the country, who were aged from two to six-and-a-half-years, in 1985-86. Mostly it was mothers (and a few fathers) who completed it with their child's teacher or nursery worker. It was also important to know how the parents and staff felt about the value of *All About Me*. On the basis of all the information, *All About Me* was revised during 1987.

All About Me is written in the first person, from the point of view of the child.

There are seven areas in *All About Me*: language; playing and learning; doing things for myself; my physical development; my health and my habits; other people and how I behave; my moods and feelings. This last, new section (not contained in other scales or schedules) explores the constellation of a young child's feelings, likes, dislikes, fears, sources of pleasure, thus reflecting a here-and-now 'snapshot' view of the young child.

Although *All About Me* adopts a developmental framework, it is not age-tied and is based on acceptance of the idea that children develop at different ages and stages, thus reducing parental anxiety and expectations regarding the 'right' age and stage when their children reach various milestones. *All About Me* aims to reflect the uniqueness of each child, by presenting a picture of the child as s/he is, now. It mostly uses an open-ended sentence completion approach with some YES/NO boxes to tick with space for comments. So parents and child can complete a sentence or statement in their own words and present a lively picture of the child at home, rather than fill in an entire page of YES/NO answers (common to some other checklist formats), which do not convey the child's individuality. The idea of parents recording their children's utterances and development is not new - an early form of an *All About Me* approach was the 'Register' kept by Richard Edgeworth and his wife on their children in the late 1770s. This was a detailed account over many months of their children's earliest development and language.

All About Me can serve as an aide-memoire for earlier as well as current development; it can be used as a basis for dialogue between parent and educator in a pre-school or infant school reception class setting; it can provide parents and educators with information on which to base play and learning programmes; it can highlight any areas of development currently causing concern to parent and/or educators, thus enabling them to take further action, including further, more detailed assessments.

Teachers and nursery workers have found a completed *All About Me* a useful complement to other forms of school or centre-based observations and record-keeping systems.

A number of schools have now introduced *All About Me* as part of their practice in profiling and record-keeping, and this could tie in with recording and reporting on progress within the National Curriculum.

Anna Francesca   2 years 3 months

Now I like to

look at books such as *The Hungry Caterpillar; the Three Bears; Pippa Little Red Riding Hood, Daisy and Nursery Rhymes*

play with puzzles such as *I don't choose puzzles very often*

play with other toys and games such as *crayons, paper, sticklebricks. I like 'helping'. I like dishing up (meals) and washing up.*

My favourite toy at the moment is *My push chair. Paddington Bear and my trike with pedals*

My favourite game at the moment is *jumping and climbing on and off the beds and on the stairs*

My favourite pretend game is *shopping*

Now I like to				**comments**
scribble		copy		I like to use felt pens and experiment with lines and shapes and colours
✓ yes	☐ no	☐ yes	☐ no	
draw		paint		
✓ yes	☐ no	✓ yes	☐ no	
play with soft toys, dolls and teddies				My dolls and teddies do all the things my baby sister does
✓ yes	☐ no			
sing, dance				
✓ yes	☐ no			
play dressing up				
☐ yes	☐ no			
use my imagination by				thinking there is a body at the bottom of the garden who is going to eat me. (Anna hears the voices of neighbours over a high hedge. I think she has connected this with Red Riding Hood!
Other things I like to do are				

Now I can

settle down to play on my own		and with other children
☐ yes ☐ not yet *somtimes*		☐ yes ☐ not yet
I like to play on my own doing *crayoning*		I like the company of other children
I like to play with (other children, adults).		I 'fit in' with the games of my older brother and his friends
☐ yes ☐ not yet		
When I play with other children we		
I like exploring and finding out about things, such as		
I am usually curious about *people I see. I want to know what they are doing. I say "whats that?" and "why?".*		

SECTION 8
Making
it work

8

*Making
Assessment
Work*

SECTION EIGHT   MAKING IT WORK

INTRODUCTION

In this section we reach the heart of the pack, and the difficult question of how we can make the process of assessment work for the benefit:

- of all children, including children with special learning needs and exceptional abilities

- of their parents

- of all the educators who work with children

Section Nine looks at the ways in which you pass on the fruits of your assessment process to others, but this section is concerned with three ways in which you can make assessment work in your own workplaces.

You will think about how you can use your assessment process to **review your provision as a whole.** You will consider how to use assessment as a way of identifying the strengths, the weaknesses, the gaps, and the inconsistencies in the curriculum you provide .

You will think about how you can use your assessment process to **plan and review the provision you make for individual children**. You will consider how to identify significant moments of learning for individual children, and build on these to shape a curriculum that matches each child's immediate concerns.

You will think about how you can use your assessment process to **identify the next steps to take in your own learning**. You will think about using your assessments of children's learning as signposts towards your own necessary learning as adults.

The purposes of this section are for you to think about how assessment can work in helping you to:

- review your provision as a whole

- plan and review the provision you make for individual children

- identify the next steps in your own learning

There are two activities in this section and you will need to do them both. In Activity 8A there are five examples of observations to discuss; you may like to choose just one or two if you do not have time for them all.

Making Assessment Work

1 hour for each observation

PREPARATION

Copies of the observation/s
Handout 8A1 (the discussion questions)
Pens and notebooks
Flip chart or large sheets of paper

Notes to Group Leaders

Before you begin work on this section, you will probably want to discuss with your group members how many of the five observations provided they want to work on, and how much time they would like to give to this activity. It is also worth considering whether the questions given for this activity could be applied to observations and assessments made by group members themselves, in their own workplaces. Using a similar format to the one on Handout 8A1 members might spend some time thinking about their own practice in **Making it Work**. This could constitute a very useful follow-up activity - or even a series of activities.

ACTIVITY 8A Contd   **Horst, Alice and James,
                              Guljeet, Bevan and Joey**

The following brief notes may help you make a selection
that suits the interests of your group members.

Horst (15m)	An observation made in the family of a toddler who is pre-occupied with how things work.
Alice (4yrs) James (3yrs)	An account of the absorbing interest shown by two children in vertical movements and marks (the 'dynamic vertical schema')
Guljeet (4 yrs)	An observation of blockplay, showing the various ways in which Guljeet is representing her experiences.
Bevan (5yrs)	A report of the play of a child tackling the technical challenges of building a house with junk box materials, and his parents' observations of play at home afterwards.
Joey (6yrs)	An observation of a child with special learning needs playing with water.

INTRODUCTION TO THE ACTIVITY

In this activity you will be able to read extracts from some
observations made by educators in a variety of settings. You
will be able to think about how they, and you, could put
these assessments to work.

The purposes of this activity are for you to use the
examples to help you:

- review the curriculum provided and think about
  what you might do next

- review the provision for individual children and
  think about what you might do next

- think about what the educator would need to
  know or learn

in order to Make Assessment Work!

ACTIVITY 8A   Horst, Alice and James,
Guljeet, Bevan and Joey

1. Working alone, read one of the observations provided, noting down your first reactions to this child's learning, and to the educator's responses.

2. In pairs or small groups think about one of the sets of questions on Handout 8A1 so that at least one group is working on each of the following:

    WHAT WAS GOING ON?

    WHAT WILL YOU DO NEXT?

    WHO WILL YOU TALK TO?

    WHAT WILL YOU WRITE DOWN?

3. Now come together in a large group and summarise your discussion on **Making it Work.** Chart your ideas on a large sheet of paper under the following headings (use a fresh sheet for the observation of each child). For example:

planning and reviewing the provision you make for a particular child

identifying the next steps in your own learning

reviewing your provision as a whole

Making 'IT' Work for Horst

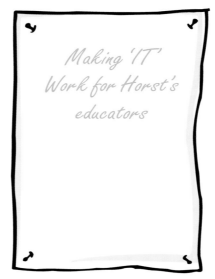

Making 'IT' Work for Horst's educators

Making 'IT' Work for all the children who play and learn with Horst

4. Repeat these stages, 1, 2 and 3, with another of the observations provided. Or you may prefer to work with your own observations of children in your work place (you might refer back to the observations you made in Section Four).

*Making
Assessment
Work*

Use some of these questions to ask yourself how you would make these observations and your assessments work for the benefit of each child, the curriculum and the educator.

WHAT WAS GOING ON?

* What parts of the observation seem most important to you? Why?

* What do you think the child may have been learning?

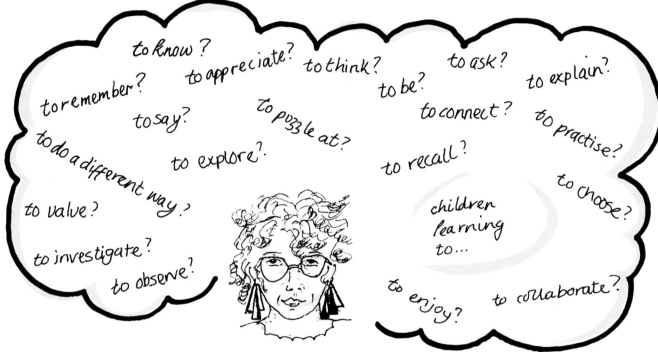

* What theoretical frameworks have given you insights into this learning? You may want to look back at Handout 7B **Formats for curriculum and assessment**.

WHAT WILL YOU DO NEXT?

* What other activities/experiences might you set up for this child?

* What materials might you choose to provide? Tomorrow? Next week?

* What experiences might you offer to all the children in the group?

* What would your next observation focus on?

* What would you be most excited to see?

* What might give you cause for concern?

* How will this observation affect your provision in other areas of your room/workplace?

* What do you need to learn more about?

Making
Assessment
Work

WHO WILL YOU TALK TO?

- What will you talk to the child about?

- When you respond to the child what form of words or what kinds of communication will you use?

- Would you show or tell the child about the observation/ record you have made? Would you invite the child's comments?

- What will you ask the child's parents about what you have observed?

- What will you tell the child's parents about the observation?

- What will you say to the other educators in the team?

WHAT WILL YOU WRITE DOWN?

If this incident happened in your workplace what could you write down:

- in the child's profile/achievement record?

- in the home/school daily diary?

- in your planning book?

- on your agenda for the next staff meeting?

- on the agenda for the next governors' meeting?

- in a letter to your MP, a local councillor, the local paper?

- in a memo to other supporting professionals?

- in your note book to remind you next time you visit the library?

- somewhere else not listed here?

Horst is 15-months-old. His family are celebrating Christmas. Just imagine, the room is full of trikes, sit and ride toys, stack and push and pull toys, and every kind of gift from all the toy shops that his adoring and thoughtful relatives have showered on this cherished and celebrated infant.

WHAT WAS HE DOING?

I noticed that the thing which really grabbed his attention for more than a fleeting moment of curiosity and to which he repeatedly returned to investigate, was the game of unplugging the Christmas tree lights. A safety socket prevented him from plugging them in again by himself, so he would appeal to an adult by offering the plug and at the same time uttering 'dah' with an assertive questioning intonation. His vocalisations and gestures clearly communicated 'I need you to put this plug in here'. This exchange developed into a regular turn-taking game. Horst enjoyed the effects of the lights coming on, but at once he would pull the plug out again.

I think his primary concern was with controlling the lighting and noting the effect of his action with the plug. Any familiar adult would do, and he soon selected the ones most willing to assist his play and the replication of his experiment.

The loving relatives (educators) watching Horst looked for other ways to extend his interest in 'making things work' or 'finding out' how objects responded to his actions. His family introduced him to:

• a wind up toy truck that moved forwards and somersaulted away from objects at the switch of a lever

• a toy lawn mower that sprayed 'grass cuttings' as it was pushed along the carpet

• a horn on his sit-and-ride car

• the pedal bin in the kitchen

HORST FOUND:

• the switch on the stereo to turn on the music

• the television control panel to turn the picture on and off (not to watch it)

• the button on the carpet cleaner to stop the noise

• the push-buttons on the telephone (the real one, not his toy one with wobbly eyes and pull-along wheels).

Horst worked hard to learn how to open the pedal bin by rocking his weight from one foot to the other to generate enough force to open it. Even though he could easily open the lid with his hands he would seek the assistance of an adult to operate the pedal. All the other toys offered by his family only received transitory attention. Horst's own discoveries seemed to be much more satisfying and pleasurable. He returned to them repeatedly and was persistently concerned with the mechanisms of these household objects.

*Making
Assessment
Work*

MAKING IT WORK

'In the nursery where I worked, I watched children playing with the range of materials available for them to explore. Alice (4 years, 5 months) and James (3 years, 11 months) were both absorbed by things that moved up and down. I watched Alice as she used the slide in the nursery garden. As she played, I described her actions to her: 'You're running up, spreading your arms, holding on to the bar. Now you're turning and running down the slide again.'

I was using my talk to reflect back her actions in language, - trying to help her represent the concept of 'up and down' symbolically, through spoken language, as well as physically, with her whole body.

Alice seemed to be interested in what I was saying but she continued her actions silently. Later that day, I watched her playing on the slide again and heard her say: 'Up the slide and down the slide again.'

While James painted vertical marks on paper, I described his actions to him as I had with Alice: 'Those are interesting marks, James. You're making up and down marks.' James smiled and made other similar marks. When he had finished his painting, I invited James to talk about it. He said: 'That's Spiderman and he's jumping from the top to right down here.' As he spoke, he made a red mark from the top to the bottom of his page.'

For more information about schemas see Handouts 3C(D) and 7A1.

What the children did

Alice demonstrated her vertical schema by:
- choosing equipment that enabled her to move up and down
- moving up and down repeatedly
- using the words 'up' and 'down'

James demonstrated his vertical schema by:
- making vertical marks in paint
- making a verbal description of his work which included the concept of 'going down'

What I did

- provided time, space and equipment
- observed her play
- matched my talk to her actions
- gave her time and opportunity to repeat her activity later the same day

- provide time, space and materials
- observed his painting
- matched my talk to his actions, using vocabulary that matched the marks he was making
- invited him to talk about his mark-making

Guljeet, aged four, is working with the hollow blocks with Levi; they make a slide with steps going up (the educator's diagram).

Guljeet organises children to go in line, and invites me to take a turn too.

'Everyone get in line. I'm going to make a photo of her on the slide.' Fetches paper and pencil. I encouraged her to look at the shapes of the bricks she has used.

G: 'I can't see it when people are on it' (waving people off). She sits down with paper and pencil.

   'Make a rectangle round there to make a photo.' Draws the slide (1) then goes to get another piece of paper and draws human figures (2) (see over).

G: 'Like the lady did outside with girls and boys.' (A photographer had taken the class photo recently).

Guljeet continues drawing: 'We have to put the boys at the bottom so they don't get mixed up ... Now I'm going to get scissors and cut it out .... Now I'm going to stick it and then I'll make tickets to go on the slide .... I'll cut the tickets and you (me!) must tell me how to write it. I want to write 'You can go on the slide.' There has been a lot of ticket making/invitation writing going on recently in child initiated play activities. I wrote out the words at Guljeet's dictation and Guljeet copies it (3) forming all the letters correctly.

Another child approaches -'Can I go on the slide?'

G: 'I doing tickets. Wait!'.... Another child tries to use the slide, 'Wait, Raji!'.... 'Levi, wait a minute!'

Raji tries again.

G: 'Raji! **wait!** a minute ....'

G: 'When I say "ready", everyone can go. People can give the ticket back and more people can go on.'

She has finished copying four tickets. She organises a ticket for each child waiting and stands by the slide.

G: 'Ticket. Slide down'. She gives a ticket to M: 'What does it say?'

G: 'You can go on the slide.'

Unfortunately the play came to an abrupt halt here with the appearance of a tray of biscuits.

MAKING IT WORK

(2)

you can go on the slide

(3)

(1)

HANDOUT 8A5　　　　　　　　　　　　　　Bevan

Bevan, aged five, had been standing around watching Stephanie who had just completed a model of her bed. He seemed very intent. I asked him if he liked Stephanie's work. He said he wanted to make something.

He went out to the junk box on the corridor and came back a few minutes later, tugging at me and demanding help with his 'stuff'. There was a polystyrene package, corrugated card packing, a foil dish, an egg box and a small carton. He asked for a large carton for his 'stuff' - he went to the caretaker and chose a large tatty carton. Then Bevan put the box on the table with the 'stuff' in it for his 'house'. He told me, 'that's the kitchen with the cooker, (polystyrene) that's the sitting room (corrugated packing) that's the table (upside-down foil dish) this is the mummy's and daddy's bed, the cot, the cupboard' (polystyrene and carton). He quickly cut a door in the side using the scissors blade like a knife. He said he wanted 'a light hanging down with four lamps'. He cut an egg box down to four sections and tried to stick it unsuccessfully to the ceiling. He repeated that he wanted it to 'hang down'. He poked a hole with the scissor blade, pushed a string through and poked a hole in the egg box. He asked for some knots. I made a large knot top and bottom for him. The light hung down impressively. Bevan did not want to go out to play. He asked for the 'flaps' to be cut off. I suggested that the box might collapse, could he use them to make it stronger? He stuck three flaps back with sellotape and cut off the fourth saying it would be in the way (using scissor blade).

At home time he insisted on taking his model home; his parents reported on further developments the next morning.

At greeting time Bevan's mother told me, 'He ceremoniously placed his house on a low table in front of the television. Bevan then fetched some of his miniature play figures and selected the mother and father from the Sylvanian family of brown rabbits and laid them on the bed. Leman Ruff of the space marines concocted meals in the polystyrene kitchen and the fearsome Boglob Ork zapped the occupants with the golden hanging lights! Well I think that was the gist of it', his mother reported cheerfully as she waved to Bevan. 'He has Boglob in his pocket for playtime, I have told him he must not take it into the classroom', she informed me. 'Bevan says he wants to make another house for Boglob to zap today, he wants lights that really go on and off. Bevan's Dad could let you have some batteries from our shop if you like' she suggested, as she hurried off to work in the family business.

Making
Assessment
Work

MAKING IT WORK

An excerpt from a time sampling observation (every 30 seconds) of Joey, aged six, playing in the water. Joey attends a Nursery Assessment Unit for children with learning difficulties. He has inherited Fragile X Syndrome and is epileptic. The severity of Joey's seizures has resulted in his treatment with drugs that may produce side effects such as mental confusion, poor control of body movements and impaired learning behaviour. In the Unit Joey reacts to the adults and children around him; this can take the form of humour, affection, verbal comment or aggression

41   Trying to take 7 Up bottle from James

42   Has obtained bottle, filling it through funnel from empty cardboard powder-paint tin

43   Emptying bottle into sink, James tries to get bottle

44   As 42

45   Blowing into crumpled bottle to expand it - then crumpling it again

46   Approaches teachers to blow into bottle

47   Standing at sink

48   Filling bottle from small shampoo bottle, turning tap on

49   Turning both taps off

50   Running water out of bottle over James' hands

51   Filling bottle from tap

52   Emptying bottle into bucket

53   Pouring from bottle into William's and James' containers

54   Snatching bottle from William but fails to get it

55   Holds bottle on bottom of sink watching bubbles come up

56   Filling and emptying bottles

57   Filling and emptying bottles

58   Filling and emptying bottles

59   Filling and emptying bottles

60   Blowing in bottle and filling from tap

61   Filling large bottle from small bottle tap on

62   Holding both bottles on bottom of sink

63   Emptying large bottle down side of sink (Deep tray containing water stands in unstopped sink to prevent disaster if taps are left running)

64   Filling small bottle from tap

65   Filling and emptying small bottle using water from sink

66   Filling and emptying small bottle using water from sink

67   Release small bottle and pours water from bucket

68   Sloshes water over side of container into sink, watches carefully

69   Sloshes water over side of container into sink, watches carefully

70   Puts plastic fish under tap and then in mouth

71   Sucks and licks plastic fish and rubs spit with finger

72   Manoeuvring fish through water, held by tail; 'Brrrrrrm, brrrrrrm, aaaah!'

Joey's educator comments that he is often to be observed 'filling things up' in sand and water play. She reflects that so far the only other opportunity for this has been in cookery sessions. She thinks Joey's play may have been enhanced and elaborated when familiar adults play with him and show him how to use the play materials. Having identified a 'filling schema' she realised that there are a wealth of possible new experiences to offer Joey.

This observation and the commentary are taken from:

Lodge D.J. (1988) *'An Analysis of the Play of Young Children with Special Educational Needs: Four Case Studies'*. Unpublished dissertation for MA University of East Anglia, School of Education.

Activity 8B   Is it working for us?

PREPARATION

Copies of Handout 8B
Group members will need to make an observation of a child in their work place and give an account of how they **Make Assessment Work.** They will need to prepare a short presentation for the rest of the group, which could include a written copy of the observation. This work will need to be done before this session begins.

This will depend on the size of the group.

In parts one and two of the activity, you may need to encourage group members to be open about the stumbling blocks to **Making Assessment Work.** It isn't always easy to decide how to extend children's learning. Sometimes assessment seems to get stuck at the observation and recording stage and doesn't develop into the curriculum.

Part three of this activity should be an enjoyable conclusion to the section when members share their successful experiences. The group will finish on a positive note, with an opportunity for team building, and for reinforcing each other's developing confidence and skills.

INTRODUCTION TO THE ACTIVITY

In your work with Horst, Alice and James, Guljeet, Bevan, and Joey you were thinking about **Making Assessment Work** for other children, in other places, in hypothetical situations. Now you will be doing it for real!

If your assessment practice ends up as a neat parcel, ready for 'passing it on', then you will only have achieved one aspect of assessment. The central purpose must be to 'make it work' for the benefit of each child, your provision as a whole, and for your staff team .... now!

The purpose of this activity are for you to:

* look at your own observations (refer to 4D)

* look at your own formats (refer to 7B)

* examine your review process to check out that assessment really does make a difference to your curriculum

* celebrate your skill and confidence in **Making It Work.**

Making Assessment Work

1. In pairs discuss your recent assessment practices in your work place. Share your struggles in **Making It Work.** Confide in your colleagues about the possibility of dead-end assessment.

It is enjoyable sharing our observations, but we run out of time deciding what to do next!

I really get stuck at this point. I can see that Grace is raging mad, and she is being disruptive – while she adjusts to her new baby sister – but I am so worried that her reading is suffering.

John is preoccupied with 'mending' all the cars … but what **is** the next step in his learning?

I am concerned about Zoe's physical development. We have lots of records of her difficulties .. but how can we/should we make the outside play area more inviting for her. We haven't really done anything about it yet, have we?

I love watching the children playing their Boglob Ork and Lemon Ruff fantasies but isn't this play becoming a bit repetitious? What are we really doing to make it more challenging?

2. Working in small groups think about the stumbling blocks to **Making It Work.** Use the statements on handout 8B to help you identify which obstacles need to be cleared from your assessment path.

3. Working in a large group share some of the success stories of **Making It Work** in your workplace. Each of you in turn will present an observation of a child and then describe how you **Made It Work.** Keep your presentation to five minutes. At the end of each presentation group members may want to comment on the significant parts of this assessment story for their own learning.

Making Assessment Work

HANDOUT 8B   Stumbling blocks

| | Can you identify with these statements? | | |
	Yes	No	Perhaps
• I must make more time to build observations into my planning.			
• I can't do it alone, we need to get together and talk.			
• I need to think about this alone for a while, (in the bath, driving the car ...), I haven't worked out why it is bugging me.			
• No more records to be added until we have reviewed and planned as a result of the last one!			
• This format is far too complicated. If we are ever going to make it work it will have to be simplified.			
• Our records are so brief a summary they don't really give us enough to go on for **Making It Work.**			
• I used to think **Making It Work** was automatic, that we did it subconsciously. Now I suppose this is really avoiding a difficult task.			
• I find it really hard to put into words what I feel, and think and know about children's learning.			
• I don't know enough about children's learning, I want to read more to gain more knowledge and understanding of **Making It Work**.			
• **Making It Work** for individual children is the hardest part. I have so many children to think of, we will **have** to share the task.			
• **Making It Work** for **me** is the hardest part. I am nervous about studying and reading. I know I am good with children, but I wasn't much good at learning at school.			
• I don't want to lose the spontaneity of the curriculum I offer.			
•			
•			
•			
and please add your own 'stumbling blocks'.			

SECTION EIGHT: MAKING IT WORK

The main themes of this section have been:

there is a clear distinction between 'MAKING IT WORK' and 'PASSING IT ON'

effective assessment supports and extends children's learning as individuals, and in groups, and helps educators identify their own learning needs

in effective assessment, parent's contributions are invited, welcomed and put to good use

there is much more to assessment than diagnosing deficits or difficulties, labelling problems, and writing copious assessment profiles

effective assessment means finding out what children have learned to know, do and feel, and then taking responsibility for a curriculum that builds on and enriches their learning.

REFERENCES

Lodge, D.J. (1988) *An analysis of the play of young children with special educational needs: four case studies* Unpublished MA dissertation, University of East Anglia School of Education.

Nutbrown, C. (1989) "Patterns in painting, patterns in play" in *Topic: Practical Applications of Research in Education* Spring NFER - Nelson (See Activity 3C).

Blenkin, G.M. and Kelly, A.V. (eds) (1992) *Assessment in Early Childhood Education.* Paul Chapman Publishing, London.

Bruce, T. (1991) *Time for Play in Early Childhood Education* Hodder & Stoughton. Chapter 8 "Practical Strategies" (especially pp 154-157).

Drummond, M.J. (1993) *Assessing Children's Learning.* David Fulton Press.

Drummond, M.J. and Nutbrown, C. (1992) 'Observing and Assessing Young Children' in Pugh G (ed) *Contemporary Issues in the Early Years: Working collaboratively for Children,* Paul Chapman Publishing, London.

Paley, V.G. (1991) *The boy who would be a helicopter* Harvard University Press.

SECTION NINE   PASSING IT ON

INTRODUCTION

In Section Eight, you considered ways in which your assessments of children's learning can be made to work for the benefit of children and educators in your own workplace. Now it is time to think about other audiences for your assessments: how can other people in other settings benefit from your knowledge and understanding? How can you most effectively pass on what you know about the children you have been assessing?

The purposes of this section are for you to:

•   think about how communication might be improved between educators by examining how you respond to assessments made by others

•   distinguish between information that is confidential, inconsequential and essential for particular audiences, so that what you pass on is worthwhile for everyone concerned

•   discuss what principles you draw on when you and your colleagues summarise all that you know about a child's learning

•   think about the ways of 'passing it on' that will be most worthwhile for the child's next educators, so that you can help them to make assessment work too

•   think about what connections are important to maintain between your workplace and another, and to make your own definition of continuity in assessment

•   discuss the importance of accounting for the value and effectiveness of your assessment practice

There are six activities in this section and it would be best to work through them in a sequence. If you are short of time, select material in 9A, 9B and 9C first, and move on to the further issues of collaboration, continuity, and accountability at a later date.

Making Assessment Work

1 hour

ACTIVITY 9A	On the receiving end

PREPARATION

Pens and paper
Flip chart sheets
Handout 5A from **In Search of Principles**, or any other written notes preserved from your work on Section Five.

Notes to Group Leaders

This activity starts on a very negative note: you may need to assure group members that they will be working towards a more positive outcome. By starting with thinking about all the ways in which 'passing it on' can go wrong, they will be more able to think constructively about ways of ensuring that it goes well.

It may also be important to reassure people that the attitudes they are exploring are all normal human responses to a complex and confusing process - that of learning how to learn from others without relinquishing one's own judgement and integrity. The purpose of the activity is to find out if any of our attitudes to each other's assessment practices may damage the children themselves. And, even more important, how to prevent that damage.

INTRODUCTION TO THE ACTIVITY

Have you ever heard a colleague - or a friend - or even yourself - say something like this?

Start with a clean slate, that's what I say

I like to make up my own mind about them

Well, her mother would say that, wouldn't she?

Children can easily get labelled

Do you remember what Tom's records said? You'd have thought he was a monster!

Other people's records can be biased

I never read the records till half term

Of course they're all perfect from that nursery

Making Assessment Work

Sometimes the pride we take in our own professional judgements can cause us, consciously or unconsciously, to undervalue the judgements of others - including educators and parents. In this activity you will be able to think about the reasons for these attitudes, to explore the implications of attitudes 'on the receiving end', and to think about how communication might be improved between those passing on, and those receiving, important information.

ACTIVITY 9A On the receiving end

1. Begin this activity by thinking about all the ways in which assessment information might be mistakenly perceived 'on the receiving end'. This is an exercise in mental ingenuity in thinking of all the possible negative responses to assessment information passed on from another source; such negative responses might range from caution ('taking it with a pinch of salt') to outright rejection ('you can't expect me to believe **that**!'). Work with a partner to list all the 'things people say' about assessments made by others.

   Try to put these ideas into the form of actual sentences or exclamations!

2. When your list has 10 or 12 items on it, exchange lists with another pair. Think about the reasons why an early years educator might have adopted each of these attitudes.

   For example:

   List the possible explanations

   Belief in one's professional judgement
   Children may change in different settings
   Caution about prejudging children
   Previous difficult experiences

   and so on ...

3. Working as a whole group, collect all the different explanations on a flip chart sheet, by taking a couple from each pair's list, until they are all used up. Note which explanations are mentioned most frequently. Refer to your list of principles developed in Section Five and think about how your principles can help you think more clearly. Use this list as an antidote to attitudes that could be harmful.

*Making
Assessment
Work*

4. Working as a whole group, select one of these explanations - preferably one that has been mentioned more than once. Now think about the possible effects on both children and educators of this attitude. You may like to group them into positive and negative effects.

For example:

Attitude Belief in one's professional judgement.

Possible positive effects	Possible negative effects
• Self-confidence	• Mistrust of others
• Ability to act on judgements for the benefit of children	• Lack of openness to different opinions
	• Early labelling of children

and so on ....

5. Conclude the discussion by working in small groups. Use a flip chart sheet to list, first, in one column, all the things you would really like to hear people say when they are on the receiving end of your assessments. Then, in a parallel column, list any possible practical strategies that might help to bring about the state of affairs you desire.

For example:

I'd like to hear	It might happen if ....
'Thank you for telling me this!'	Face to face meetings No jargon

Just wait till you get Darren's little brother Adolf

ACTIVITY 9B   Principles for passing it on

PREPARATION

Pens and notebooks
Flip chart sheets and felt tip pens

about 45 minutes

Notes to Group Leaders

In this activity group members will think about 'passing it on' to parents, other educators and supporting specialists, in order to establish the principles that underlie worthwhile practice. Group members may need some support in moving on from concrete details and personal practice to a more abstract discussion of principles.

INTRODUCTION TO THE ACTIVITY

Observations and assessments are part and parcel of living and working with young children. Much of what we see and record we keep to ourselves - in our memories, in a shared diary, in a personal jotter. But we also pass on a great deal of information, both formally and informally, regularly and continuously, week by week, month by month, to a wide variety of people - parents, nursers, health visitors, support teachers, Portage workers, childminders .... the list is almost endless.

In this activity you will be able to

*   think about the kinds of information you need to select for different audiences

*   consider the rights of parents and children to confidentiality

*   create a list of principles for sharing your assessments with all the people who support your work with children

*Making
Assessment
Work*

PASSING IT ON

1. Working in twos or threes, preferably with people from your own workplace, select a child whom you all know as the subject for this activity. If this isn't possible, work with people from a similar setting, and either select a child whom one of you has talked about before, or select a child who is causing one of you concern, so that the discussion may be useful in other ways (as a chance to talk over these concerns). For the purposes of describing this activity, let's call the child Susan.

    Work together to write a list of all the people who will be the audiences for your regular and continuous observations and assessments of Susan. Think about your spoken communication with these people as well as any written information you give them. Look ahead as well as at the present. Include family members, as well as other educators and professionals. Does everyone on the list need to know the same things from you?

2. Now for each person on the list, note down

    *   three items of essential information/reflection/judgement that you believe she or he really needs to know

    *   three items of inconsequential information that need not be passed on to this particular person

    *   three items that might be strictly confidential to the key worker or staff team

    Some differences are easy to distinguish. For example, Susan's sudden attack of diarrhoea one afternoon will only interest certain audiences; and her continuing uncontrollable fear of thunderstorms will not be news to Susan's parents/carers, but might be important for someone meeting Susan for the first time. Susan's special interest in and knowledge of cats could be worthwhile information for everyone who works with her.

3. After your discussion about 'Susan', work as a whole group to ask yourselves WHY certain kinds of information seem to be appropriate for certain audiences. Then identify a few general principles for passing on your assessments to other people. Add these principles to the list you made in activity 5A.

Making
Assessment
Work

ACTIVITY 9C — Summing it up

PREPARATION

Flip chart sheets, felt tip pens and blutak
List of principles developed in Activities 5A and 9B

1 hour, 15 minutes

Notes to Group Leaders

This is quite a long and challenging activity, based on the intensive use of 'why' questions. Group members will need encouragement to keep on questioning each other: the temptation will be to slip into a description of 'how we do it now', rather than thinking about the reasons for doing it in any particular way.

To be most useful, the activity should be done in small groups of people from the same workplace, or similar settings. This will help group members to make connections between the summative assessment they are describing, and the summative assessments they actually make.

At the end of the activity, you will need to collect up members' written notes for copying and distribution at the next meeting. You may need to organise a follow-up session so that members can review their own practice in summative assessment in relation to their work on this activity.

INTRODUCTION TO THE ACTIVITY

In the last activity you looked at the ways in which early years educators pass on information, regularly and continuously, to a whole range of different people, both professionals and non-professionals. Now it is time to consider the rather different process of passing on what amounts to a summary of everything you know about a child's learning and development. (This form of assessment is sometimes called 'summative assessment'). This summary is what you pass on when a child leaves your workplace for another setting; it is the best account you can give of what each child does, knows, feels and understands - but it cannot ever be complete; it can only be a selection of what you know.

The purposes of this activity are for you to:

* discuss and define the characteristics of a worthwhile summary of a child's learning and development

* think about the process of selecting information for this summary: what to include and why; what to leave out and why

* consider how best to include three different perspectives: the child's, the parents' and the educators'

1.　Working as a whole group, write on a large flip chart sheet as many words as you can to describe what you think a summary of a child's learning and development should or should not look like. Don't discuss the precise meaning of every word just yet: first collect as many ideas as you can. And don't - yet - discuss whether or not you agree with every idea that is suggested.

Try to collect at least 20 or 30 words or phrases

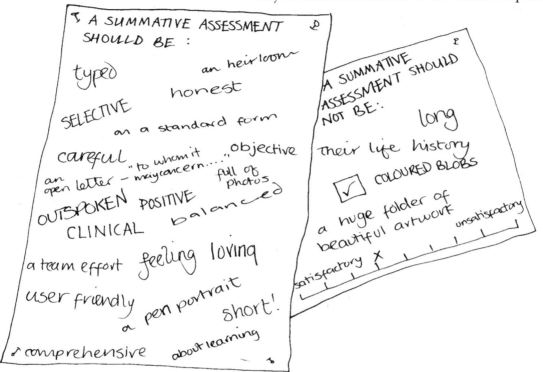

2.　When the flip chart sheet - or sheets - is crowded with words and phrases, spend a few minutes checking the precise meaning of any terms that aren't quite clear.

Next, work in pairs, if possible with someone from your own workplace, to look more closely at each word on the list, and think about WHY this is a desirable characteristic of a completed assessment process. Make sure that you ask 'why?' about every word on the list, even if it seems obvious. It is often easier just to nod, and agree with one another, than to check out each other's thinking, but it is sometimes worthwhile to force oneself, and one's partner, to spell out the ideas that we normally take for granted.

Make a list of the essential characteristics of a worthwhile summary of your assessments.

There may be some ideas on the list that you want to reject. This is an important step to take, so be sure you know WHY.

Making Assessment Work

3.　In small groups of four or six, compare your lists. Be sure to ask each other WHY about any differences between the lists.

ACTIVITY 9C	Summing it up

Now check to see that your lists include the following three elements:

1. THE VOICE OF THE CHILD

*   The child's own self appraisal, which may be different from yours.....

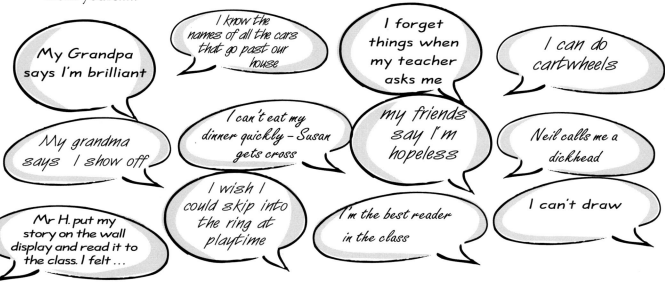

Which of these imaginary comments would you include? Why? Add some more examples from your own experience.

2. THE VOICE OF PARENTS

•   The parents' knowledge and feelings about the child's achievements, and their concerns about their child's learning and development (which may be different from yours).....

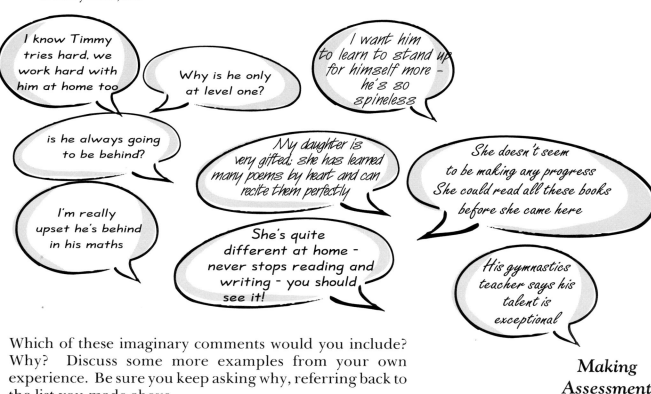

Which of these imaginary comments would you include? Why? Discuss some more examples from your own experience. Be sure you keep asking why, referring back to the list you made above.

Making Assessment Work

3. THE VOICE OF THE EDUCATOR

- Your summary of the most vital and the most relevant information about what the child does, and knows, and feels and understands and is learning now.

Joey is persistently concerned with water; his preferred activity is water play of every variety – puddles, taps, & the paddling pool, anything. He does get very wet, because his interest is so intense & he explores what's happening so actively. He is especially interested in the different ways that water moves – and how <u>he</u> can <u>make</u> it move.

Frances loves to watch the pigeons from her buggy. She is fascinated by their movements and has learned to anticipate the patterns of their flight. She searches for them with her gaze in the places where she has learned that they perch. She concentrates for longer and longer periods.....

Do these imaginary extracts match the words and phrases on the list you have made about 'Summative Assessment'? Look back at your earlier lists of principles, and discuss whether you need to change them, or add to them, to help you in the process of making summative assessments.

4. You will now be able to use all your work on this activity to update, create, or extend your procedures for making a summary of assessment. You may need to arrange a follow-up meeting to look at your present practice and check it against:

- the principles developed in activities 5A and 9B

- all the desirable and essential characteristics of a completed summary of assessment that you identified in this activity.

Making Assessment Work

ACTIVITY 9D   Working together

PREPARATION

Pens and notebooks
Copies of the Handout

1 hour

Notes to Group Leaders

This activity is probably most suitable for those who regularly transfer children into a nursery class, four plus unit, a reception class, or the next class in the primary school.

The activity requires the use of the imagination, planning activities and exchanges that may never happen. Sometimes the excitement of thinking imaginatively in this way can distract people from the overall purpose of the activity. You may find you occasionally have to remind the small groups that they are trying to find ways in which 'passing it on' can work for the maximum benefit of all concerned, for children, for parents and for the educators themselves.

INTRODUCTION TO THE ACTIVITY

So far in this section you have considered the process of passing on information about individual children. In this activity you will be able to think about the ways in which you can make your assessments of a number of children most worthwhile for another group of educators.

The purposes of this activity are for you to:

* consider how you might find out more about the settings and the educators to whom your children transfer

* discuss what they might want to learn from you, about your workplace

* think about some of the feelings that might be aroused by working more closely with another group of educators, trying to understand each other's practices and principles

*Making
Assessment
Work*

1. Imagine that you and your colleagues have been given a whole training day, without the children, to spend time on improving the process of 'passing it on' from your workplace to the setting to which your children transfer. The staff of that setting have also been given up to a day to spend with you, if you need it. Your task in this activity is to plan the day, describing your intentions, the activities you will set up, the questions you will ask, the difficulties you might meet, and the outcomes that you would hope to realise.

2. Work in a small group throughout this activity, preferably with colleagues from your own workplace.

   Write, first, a list of what you hope the day will offer you, using the Handout.

   DURING THE DAY, WE WILL BE ABLE TO:

   Make the list as detailed, specific, practical and imaginative as you can. For example, if you would really like simply to watch some children you know well during a whole morning in their new setting, then this is the time to say so. Or, if you prefer talking to an individual, rather than working with a whole staff group, specify your need for some one-to-one discussion with a particular member of staff.

3. Next write a list of your questions for the staff group you will meet, so that you can learn about their work, using the Handout.

   WE WILL ASK THEM ABOUT:

   Remember the focus of the day is 'passing it on', but in the process of thinking about this, you may want to ask questions about a wide variety of issues - about almost any aspect of the curriculum, for example, or about systems of observation and record keeping, or about the place of the National Curriculum in the new setting, or about parents and educators working together. There is no limit to what you might want to learn.

4. Now think about the sorts of activities observations, discussions, reading time, group work, and so on that you think will best help you achieve your intended learning. Write out your plan of the day, using the Handout.

   PLAN OF THE DAY

   Whatever else happens on this imaginary day, you and your colleagues will experience a range of emotions. Spend a few minutes talking about these, acknowledging that some less than ecstatic feelings are probably inevitable. Think about the possibility that anxiety and apprehension, in moderation, may actually help you get more from the day's activities.

5. Think about what you hope will be the outcomes of the day for your colleagues in the other institution/setting. Try to think of yourselves as collaborating in a shared learning project. What do you want to help them to learn about your assessment practice?

   WE WILL TRY TO SHOW THEM: ....

HANDOUT 9D   **Working together**

DURING THE DAY WE WILL BE ABLE TO .... Make a list:

DURING THE DAY WE WILL ASK THEM ABOUT .... Make a list:

PLAN OF THE DAY .... Design a programme:

WE WILL TRY TO SHOW THEM .... Make a list

45 minutes

| Activity 9E | What is continuity? |

PREPARATION

Pens and notebooks
Large sheets of paper

Notes to Group Leaders

You may want to collect the individual sentences written at the end of the activity to form into a combined handout for distribution at your next meeting.

INTRODUCTION TO THE ACTIVITY

The dictionary definition of continuity is 'uninterrupted connection'. This rather concise description has two strands to it: the idea of interruption, and the idea of connection. When we talk about continuity between one form of early years experience and another, we are bound to accept that some kind of interruption is inevitable at moments of transition. What we can then do is focus on connections, and explore what it is, or might be, possible to achieve by way of establishing 'uninterrupted connections'.

The purposes of this activity are for you to

* distinguish between the necessary interruptions and the essential connections between your workplace and another one

* develop a personal definition of continuity

1. Working in small groups of three of four, make two lists. In the first list, note down all those aspects of your provision that cannot possibly be continuous, that must suffer interruption at transition - for example, the staff, the room itself, the furniture - and many more. In the second list, note all those aspects of your provision that could possibly be made to connect smoothly with the same aspect of another setting. Head your lists:

INTERRUPTIONS

For example:
- staff/personnel
- friendship groups

and

POSSIBLE CONNECTIONS

For example:
- languages spoken
- forms of address - Mrs Stone or Sally?
- working with parents
- individual learning patterns
- similar activities: for example, block play, natural materials
- significant recent learning

2. Show your lists to another small group, and talk about any substantial differences between the lists. Speculate about the reasons for these differences.

3. Look at the interruptions and ask yourselves:

- Is this interruption relevant to our assessment practice?

- Will this interruption affect the way in which our assessments are received?

- Is there anything we can do about it?

- Does this interruption affect the way in which we put together our summative assessments? Should it?

Look at the items on the connections list and ask yourselves:

- Is this connection relevant to our assessment practice? If it is, then do we use it to our benefit?

4. Bring the discussion to a close by discussing whether any items on the interruptions list could or should be moved over to the connections list, in order to make your assessment practice more effective.

5. End the activity by working on your own, writing a short definition of one aspect of continuity that is important for you. Select one item from the connections list, and write a sentence that explains why this kind of continuity is important for your assessment practice.

Read your individual sentences round the group, commenting briefly on each one. The group leader might collect the sentences together to make a combined handout for the next meeting.

Making Assessment Work

1 hour

ACTIVITY 9F	Being accountable

PREPARATION

Pens and paper
Large sheets of paper, felt tip pens

Notes to Group Leaders

The subject of accountability is a big and complex one - too big and too complex to be dealt with comprehensively here. The purpose of this activity is not, therefore, to examine every aspect of the subject, or to review the multitude of ways in which early years educators are accountable for their work. This activity is designed to focus on just one aspect of accountability: the part that assessment can play in it. And the activity focuses on just one possible form of accountability in which assessment can play a part. This is not to suggest that an 'open evening' is the only way in which early years educators can be seen to be accountable: this imaginary event has been selected simply to illustrate the principle that is at the heart of the activity: the necessary relationship between accountability and assessment practice. The group leader will need to emphasise the way in which the activity illustrates this principle, rather than exhausts all its possibilities.

INTRODUCTION TO THE ACTIVITY

So far in this section you have been thinking about some very specific audiences to whom you pass the fruits of your assessment practice: the parents and other professionals who are your partners in the care and education of young children. You have thought about ways in which passing it on can make the work of other educators more effective. But there is another reason why all early years educators need to be confident and articulate about their assessment practice. All of us who work with young children are accountable for what we do: to those who fund our work, to our management committees, to our employers, to our board of governors, to our colleagues in other parts of the school, to our community organisations, and so on.

The purpose of this activity is for you to:

*   explore the relationship between accountability and assessment

*   discuss one way in which you and your colleagues might be accountable, by drawing on what you learn through your assessment practice to justify and explain your work

ACTIVITY 9F — Being accountable

1. Imagine that your local community is holding an Open Week. You and your colleagues have volunteered to open your doors during the week to interested members of the community. One of the events you have started to plan is an 'open evening' about one aspect of your practice. You have designed posters and publicity leaflets and the response has been very positive. Twenty people, some of them parents, but not all, will be attending an evening session of about one-and-a-half hours, to take part in a workshop about .... the subject matter is for you to choose, because for the purposes of this activity, it isn't the most important thing. You are going to select an area of your practice that you have observed and developed recently, and use it as a way of exploring the part that your assessments can play in the exercise of accountability.

   Work with a small group of your colleagues to choose a focus for your work:

   - Science in the nursery school?
   - Technology in the playgroup?
   - First steps to reading in the day nursery?
   - The development of self-image in family day care?

2. Once you have selected a title for your 'open evening', work together to plan a programme. Include opportunities to talk about: What you do ... and How you do it ... and Why you do it. Make a rough sketch of how you might divide up the time.

3. Now concentrate on why you work in this way. In explaining to your audience the purposes of your work, you will also want to show how effective you are in achieving those purposes. This is where assessment comes in. It is your assessments of children's learning and development that can show the world how your **practice** results in the **children's learning.**

   Make a list of 'why' questions your imaginary audience might ask about your practice. Now think about how you would want to answer each of these questions, drawing on your observations and assessments of children. Include examples of children with exceptional gifts and special learning needs.

Write up the results of this discussion on a large sheet, so that you can talk about it to the rest of the group. Use the format shown on this page:

> THEY WILL WANT TO KNOW....

Why.........
Why.....
why.....
why.....

> SO WE TELL THEM ABOUT....

Shafiq....
Jack....
Yukio....
Teresa & Chris...

Making Assessment Work

4.   When your sheet is complete, work with the whole group to compare, contrast, discuss and, possibly, disagree.

5.   After some time in the whole group, return to your small group of colleagues and think about the following questions:

    •   Are there some parts of your assessment practice that you have not mentioned in this exercise? Why?

    •   Are some parts of your practice very much more useful for this exercise than others? Why?

    •   Does this exercise suggest any ways in which you might need to modify your practice?

    •   Does this activity suggest ways in which you might draw on your assessment practice more fully in other forms of accountability?

Review

SECTION NINE: PASSING IT ON

The main themes of this section have been:

Effective practice in 'passing it on' is the result of thinking about
   what to pass on,
   how to do it, and
   why other educators need to know what we offer them.

'Passing it on' is worthwhile when practice is based on principles that include trust, confidentiality, respect, and the paramount interests of the child.

'Passing it on' is effective when it includes the most significant and recent information about each child, from three perspectives; the child's, the parents' and the educators'.

FURTHER READING

Blenkin, G. and Kelly, V. (1992) *Assessment in Early Childhood Education.* Paul Chapman Publishing

Pugh, G. and De'Ath, E. (1989) *Working towards partnership in the early years.* National Children's Bureau.

Watt, J. and Flett, M. (1985) *Continuity in Early Education: The Role of Parents.* Department of Education. Aberdeen University.